Yours Always

Letters of
Longing

Edited by
**Eleanor
Bass**

ICON

This edition published in the UK in 2018
by Icon Books Ltd,
Omnibus Business Centre,
39–41 North Road, London N7 9DP
email: info@iconbooks.com
www.iconbooks.com

First published in the UK in 2017
by Icon Books Ltd

Sold in the UK, Europe and Asia
by Faber & Faber Ltd,
Bloomsbury House,
74–77 Great Russell Street,
London WC1B 3DA or their agents

Distributed in the UK, Europe and Asia
by Grantham Book Services, Trent Road,
Grantham NG31 7XQ

Distributed in the USA by
Publishers Group West,
1700 Fourth Street, Berkeley, CA 94710

Distributed in Canada
by Publishers Group Canada,
76 Stafford Street, Unit 300
Toronto, Ontario M6J 2S1

Distributed in Australia
and New Zealand
by Allen & Unwin Pty Ltd,
PO Box 8500, 83 Alexander Street,
Crows Nest, NSW 2065

Distributed in South Africa
by Jonathan Ball, Office B4,
The District, 41 Sir Lowry Road,
Woodstock 7925

Distributed in India
by Penguin Books India,
7th Floor, Infinity Tower – C,
DLF Cyber City,
Gurgaon 122002, Haryana

ISBN: 978-1-78578-316-6

Typeset in Dante by Marie Doherty

Printed and bound in the UK by
Clays Ltd, St Ives plc

For Nick

Eleanor Bass is a freelance researcher and writer. Having previously read Theology at the University of Cambridge, she obtained her doctorate in English Literature from King's College London in 2015. Her academic interests include life writing, letter writing and the writing of wartime. Eleanor lives in South-East London with her husband and daughter.

CONTENTS

EDITORIAL NOTE

Letters come in all shapes, sizes and degrees of legibility. It has therefore been necessary to exercise some editorial privileges in presentation.

Where applicable, I have standardised the date and place headings. When there is uncertainty over the precise date of a letter, or over a specific word within a letter, this is indicated by the use of square brackets. I have corrected spelling and, on rare occasions, grammatical errors, where these interfere with the readability of the text.

In many instances letters have been abridged, or an extract from a longer letter presented. Abridgements, which vary in length from a number of words or sentences to one or more paragraphs, are indicated by the insertion of '…'. Where a particularly lengthy portion of text has been removed this is signalled by '…' on a separate line.

Full details of the sources of letters can be found in the 'Sources, Copyright and Thanks' section on page 187.

INTRODUCTION

In Classical mythology Eros, God of Love, was not always benevolent. In the story of Apollo and Daphne he employs his powers to painful effect. Angered by Apollo's arrogance as an archer, Eros trains his arrow upon him, causing Apollo to fall passionately in love with the chaste nymph Daphne. The capricious Eros then shoots Daphne with another arrow – lead-tipped and blunt – that is guaranteed to repel all thoughts of love. In his fervour Apollo chases Daphne who, moments before being caught in his embrace, transforms into a laurel tree. Still gripped by desire, Apollo caresses the branches of the tree as if they were the limbs of his beloved.

The feverish longing of unrequited love has, it would seem, plagued mankind from ancient times. Stories of love's frustrations and disappointments have proved a staple in Western literature: from courtly tales of knights labouring valorously to win the regard of a remote and often disdainful lady, through the complicated webs of unreciprocated love favoured by Shakespeare, and the dangerous and seductive face of love revealed by the Romantic poets, to the extended exploration of love's challenges in novels of the Victorian and modern periods. The cultural history of love thus buttresses the well-known contention, originating in Shakespeare's *A Midsummer Night's Dream*, that 'the course of true love never did run smooth'. Romance favours lovers with the heady experiences of emotional fulfilment, sexual delight and unprecedented joy in life, yet simultaneously opens the door to despair.

Like love stories, the writing of love letters has a long heritage. Over the course of millennia, letters have allowed communication between lovers separated by circumstance and have provided an outlet for love's intensities of emotion – whether adulation and infatuation, or frustration and complaint. The letters collected in this book span many periods; the oldest dates from the medieval age, the most recent from the twentieth century. The writers and recipients of these letters are also varied; they include philosophers and scientists, politicians and royalty, novelists, poets and stars of stage and screen. The collection is organised so as to draw out resonances between their diverse stories. Thus the entries slip back and forth across history, loosely grouped according to the type of romantic experiences, emotions and circumstances being expressed. They illuminate the uneven path of love – from hairline fractures that emerge in the everyday routine to tectonic shifts of lovers' affections. In their expression of troubled love, these letters reveal not only the personal struggles faced by a host of prominent figures, but the complexity of love: the multitudinous ways in which romance can be derailed and love go wrong.

The first section of the book begins with the relentless tug of unrequited love. Letters expose the vulnerability inherent in loving without being loved in return. Yet there are also notes of self-preservation within these pages, manifesting sometimes as anger towards the beloved, sometimes as stoicism towards the dictates of fate. A less definitive uncertainty in love then emerges in two sets of courtship letters, written centuries apart, in which one party withholds their consent to marry. A further interesting example of reticence towards marriage (though one not included in this book) can be found in the letters of D.H. Lawrence to his lover Frieda Weekley. Lawrence was not in any way unsure in his desire to marry Frieda; rather, 'like the old knights', he required a period of reflection – 'a sort of vigil with myself' – ahead of the momentous change. Towards the end of this section the theme of uneven or imbalanced affection asserts itself. In these instances one party emerges as more devoted, more invested, than the other; the letters lay bare the hurt occasioned by misaligned expectations, thoughtlessness and neglect.

Focus then shifts, in the book's second section, to letters expressive of damaged, broken and thwarted love. A number of the letters illustrate how relationships may be attacked from within, warping under the pressure of partners' ill-matched needs and expectations. Others reveal couplings more thoroughly in the midst of collapse, eroded by instances of betrayal or dissipating affection. Moral and religious misgivings emerge as the primary source of strife in a number of the love affairs represented, while societal strictures of various kinds inhibit and on occasion devastate others. Outside of this collection, the impact of specific social mores upon romantic love can be observed in some of the oldest surviving love letters in the English language, those exchanged between John Paston and Margery Brews in 1476–77. Despite Margery's assurance in her letters that financial concerns are of little importance to her ('For if you had not half the livelihood that you have, and if I had to do the greatest labour that any woman alive might, I would not forsake you'), parental disharmony over the size of her dowry presented a material stumbling block to the couple's intention to marry.

The last two entries in this collection square up to the greatest challenge posed to romantic love: the inevitability of death. The first is taken from the wartime correspondence of Vera Brittain and Roland Leighton who, in 1915 with a battle looming, rushed to exchange some parting words. There are many other instances of letters penned under the descending pall of death, one famous example being the unfinished letter of Horatio Nelson to Emma Hamilton, written from the *Victory* during the Battle of Trafalgar. So too, a surviving lover may turn to the act of letter-writing as a means of reconnecting with their beloved or reflecting upon their loss. In a sixteenth-century Korean letter discovered resting on the mummified remains of its intended recipient, a grief-wracked wife cries out to her husband, 'How could you go ahead of me? … Please take me where you are.' The final entry in this collection is a poem by Ted Hughes, published almost fifty years after his estranged wife Sylvia Plath's death, in which he revisits the night of her suicide.

Love letters are potent. They breathe. They speak. They can arouse, comfort, enamour. They can also cut deep. This potency is captured in Sylvia Plath's poem 'Burning the Letters', written only a month after her discovery of Hughes' affair with Assia Wevill. The poem depicts a woman standing in the drizzling rain, watching a stash of old love letters burn. Since their initial, loving inception these letters have become menacing 'white fists', the postmarks sinister 'eyes'. They are hooked, cringing entities; 'papers that breathe like people'. It is with relief that she relegates them to the fire, rendering them blind and silencing their chatter.

One of the draws of love letters is precisely this enlivened, almost embodied quality – the way they pitch-fork the reader into the midst of vital, unfolding relationships. The words lovers write to each other are part of their love; they contribute to the texture of that attachment and fashion its future course. Reading other people's love letters is an intimate, perhaps intrusive pastime; yet it is also enriching. It provides access to the personal and emotional hinterland of some of history's great names. It reveals how, at specific moments in time, individuals responded to millennia-long traditions around love and its expression. In the case of literary figures, it demonstrates another dimension of their writerly identity and frequently offers intriguing biographical insight into their published works.

Above all, love letters teach us something of love. They demonstrate not only the many trajectories of romance, but the staggering variability of human nature; the different ways of understanding, navigating, sustaining, enduring and renouncing the experience of love. In the pages that follow, love affairs emerge as lived, evolving entities, played out in every corner of the lover's life and psyche. The letters provide a privileged glimpse into these elusive worlds of experience, and prompt the reader to reflect upon their own romantic journey – however rough the terrain.

UNREQUITED
AND UNEQUAL LOVE

CHARLOTTE BRONTË
TO PROFESSOR CONSTANTIN HÉGER

Charlotte Brontë 1816–1855; Constantin Héger 1809–1896

———◦◦◦———

Charlotte Brontë acknowledges the potency of letters in her novel *Villette*, when she has protagonist Lucy Snowe surreptitiously bury, in a sealed glass jar, precious letters from a man whom she loves who does not love her back. A degree of mystery has surrounded the letters Charlotte herself wrote to her former teacher, Professor Héger. Only four remain, penned during 1844–45, from what would appear a longer correspondence. Three of those four have been torn into pieces and reassembled.

Charlotte first met Monsieur Héger during her sojourn as a student of languages at the *Pensionnat Héger* in Brussels, which she attended alongside her sister Emily in 1842, and again as an assistant governess in 1843–44. Having grown up in the weaving village of Haworth on the edge of the Yorkshire moors, these trips offered the exhilaration of new surroundings and the opportunity for learning that Charlotte craved. Departing the *Pensionnat* in January 1844, she wrote mournfully to her good friend Ellen Nussey: 'I think however long I live I shall not forget what the parting with Monsr. Héger cost me'.

Charlotte had not, however, been immediately enamoured. In a letter to Ellen dated May 1842 she described 'a man of power as to mind but very choleric and irritable in temperament – a little, black, ugly being'. Over time her initial impression altered. An enthusiastic educator, Héger was at pains to stretch the Brontë girls; he gifted books, provided extended commentary upon their work, and troubled himself over their pronunciation of French. It is conceivable that mutual attraction may have entered into the acquaintance between Charlotte and Monsieur Héger, yet this remains conjecture. More certain is the deepening devotion Charlotte felt towards her '*maître*' (master), as expressed in the letters she wrote to him on her return to Britain. Héger, however, was married with five children, and apparently disinclined to maintain this correspondence.

Writing to the professor in French, Charlotte clings to her proficiency in the language as a means of nurturing the connection between them. She keeps him abreast of her progress and candidly explains that 'I love French for your sake with all my heart and soul'. Respect for her former teacher slips repeatedly into a more pining, infatuated tone, and emotion escalates with each letter. The first, while peppered with expressions of her regard, is conversational. The second is brief, yet gently demanding of his consideration. The third speaks of her hurt at having received no word from him, of 'unbearable' suffering and 'dreadful' uncertainty. The fourth is the saddest; it laments her failed attempts to forget him, frankly acknowledging the humiliating aspect of such a lopsided affection.

Charlotte's attachment to Monsieur Héger was fostered by the uncertainties she faced on her return from Brussels. She was unsure of her future direction in life – torn between the possibilities of teaching and writing, and conflicted in her desire to care for her ageing father and to broaden her horizons. With the immediate success of *Jane Eyre*, published in 1847, Charlotte's opportunities would significantly increase; trips to London, a professional persona, and the acquaintance of other literary figures would feed her longing for stimulating and varied experience. Thus these letters – full of pained, sometimes desperate pleas for Héger's attention – provide a disarmingly intimate insight into the interior life of a young woman still poised on the brink of literary renown.

∽

24 July 1844

Monsieur,

... I am very pleased that the school-year is nearly over and that the holidays are approaching. – I am pleased on your account, Monsieur – for I am told that you are working too hard ... For that reason I refrain from uttering a single complaint for your long silence ... Ah, Monsieur! I once wrote you a letter that was less than reasonable, because sorrow was at my heart; but I shall do so no more. – I shall try to be selfish no longer; and even while I look upon your letters as one of the greatest felicities known to me, I shall await the receipt of them in patience until it pleases you and suits you to send me any ...

I greatly fear that I shall forget French, for I am firmly convinced that I shall see you again some day ... and then I should not wish to remain dumb before you ... To avoid such a misfortune I learn every day by heart half a page of French from a book written in a familiar style: and I take pleasure in learning this lesson, Monsieur; as I pronounce the French words it seems to me as if I were chatting with you.

I have just been offered a situation as first governess in a large school in Manchester ... I cannot accept it, for in accepting it I should have to leave my father ...

… There is nothing I fear so much as idleness, the want of occupation, inactivity, the lethargy of the faculties: when the body is idle, the spirit suffers painfully.

I should not know this lethargy if I could write. Formerly I passed whole days and weeks and months in writing … but now my sight is too weak to write … Otherwise do you know what I should do, Monsieur? – I should write a book, and I should dedicate it to my literature-master – to the only master I ever had – to you, Monsieur …

Goodbye, Monsieur,

Your grateful pupil

C. Bronte

I have not begged you to write to me soon as I fear to importune you – but you are too kind to forget that I wish it all the same … If, then, I received a letter, and if I thought that you had written it out of pity – I should feel deeply wounded.

∽

24 October 1844

Monsieur,

I am in high glee this morning … It is because a gentleman of my acquaintance is going to Brussels, and has offered to take charge of a letter for you …

I am not going to write a long letter; in the first place, I have not the time – it must leave at once; and then, I am afraid of worrying you. I would only ask of you if you heard from me at the beginning of May and again in the month of August? For six months I have been awaiting a letter from

Monsieur – six months' waiting is very long, you know! However, I do not complain, and I shall be richly rewarded for a little sorrow if you will now write a letter and give it to this gentleman – or his sister – who will hand it to me without fail.

... the remembrances of your kindnesses will never fade from my memory, and as long as that remembrance endures the respect with which it has inspired me will endure likewise.

Your very devoted pupil,

C. Bronte

∾

8 January 1845

Mr. Taylor has returned. I asked him if he had a letter for me. 'No; nothing.' 'Patience,' said I – 'his sister will be here soon.' Miss Taylor has returned. 'I have nothing for you from Monsieur Héger,' says she; 'neither letter nor message.'

Having realised the meaning of these words, I said to myself what I should say to another similarly placed; 'You must be resigned, and above all do not grieve at a misfortune which you have not deserved.' I strove to restrain my tears, to utter no complaint.

But when one does not complain, when one seeks to dominate oneself with a tyrant's grip, the faculties start in rebellion, and one pays for external calm with an internal struggle that is almost unbearable.

Day and night I find neither rest nor peace. If I sleep I am disturbed by tormenting dreams in which I see you, always severe, always grave, always incensed against me.

Forgive me then, Monsieur, if I adopt the course of writing to you again. How can I endure life if I make no effort to ease its sufferings?

I know that you will be irritated when you read this letter. You will say once more that I am hysterical – that I have black thoughts, &c. So be it, Monsieur … All I know is that I cannot, that I will not, resign myself to lose wholly the friendship of my master. I would rather suffer the greatest physical pain than always have my heart lacerated by smarting regrets. If my master withdraws his friendship from me entirely I shall be altogether without hope; if he gives me a little – just a little – I shall be satisfied – happy; I shall have reason for living on, for working.

… You will tell me perhaps – 'I take not the slightest interest in you, Mademoiselle Charlotte. You are no longer an inmate of my House; I have forgotten you.'

Well, Monsieur, tell me so frankly. It will be a shock to me. It matters not. It would be less dreadful than uncertainty.

I shall not re-read this letter. I send it as I have written it. Nevertheless, I have a hidden consciousness that some people, cold and commonsense, in reading it would say – 'She is talking nonsense.' I would avenge myself on such persons in no other way than by wishing them one single day of the torments which I have suffered for eight months. We should then see if they would not talk nonsense too.

One suffers in silence so long as one has the strength so to do, and when that strength gives out one speaks without too carefully measuring one's words.

I wish Monsieur happiness and prosperity.

C.B.

∽

18 November [1845]

Monsieur,

The six months of silence have run their course … I may therefore write to you without failing in my promise.

… I tell you frankly that I have tried meanwhile to forget you … I have done everything; I have sought occupations; I have denied myself absolutely the pleasure of speaking about you … but I have been able to conquer neither my regrets nor my impatience. That, indeed, is humiliating – to be unable to control one's own thoughts, to be the slave of a regret, of a memory, the slave of a fixed and dominant idea which lords it over the mind. Why cannot I have just as much friendship for you, as you for me – neither more nor less? Then should I be so tranquil, so free …

Monsieur, I have a favour to ask of you: when you reply to this letter, speak to me a little of yourself, not of me; for I know that if you speak of me it will be to scold me … Your last letter was stay and prop to me – nourishment to me for half a year. Now I need another and you will give it me; not because you bear me friendship – you cannot have much – but because you are compassionate of soul and you would condemn no one to prolonged suffering to save yourself a few moments' trouble. To forbid me to write to you, to refuse to answer me, would be to tear from me my only joy on earth, to deprive me of my last privilege … So long as I believe you are pleased with me, so long as I have hope of receiving news from you, I can be at rest and not too sad. But when a prolonged and gloomy silence seems to threaten me with the estrangement of my master …

then a fever claims me – I lose appetite and sleep – I pine
away …

    C. Bronte

… You will see by the defects in this letter that I am forgetting
the French language – yet I read all the French books I can
get … I love French for your sake with all my heart and soul.

WINSTON CHURCHILL TO MURIEL WILSON

Winston Churchill 1874–1965; Muriel Wilson 1871–1964

―――――◦◦◦◦―――――

Winston Churchill is remembered for his stirring oratory and flinty determination as Prime Minister of Great Britain during the Second World War. He dedicated himself to a political career in 1899, winning his first seat as Conservative MP for Oldham in 1900. He was also a talented writer, publishing five books by the age of twenty-six. Yet these were not the only passions that stirred the young Churchill's blood; he had his sights firmly fixed on matrimony, and was attracted to a number of beautiful society women during his twenties.

As his career began to gather steam, however, Winston's private life was stalling. By 1904 he had suffered two failed marriage proposals. The first woman to capture his heart was flirtatious beauty Pamela Plowden, whom he met in India; the second, glamorous American actress Ethel Barrymore. At the age of twenty-nine, Churchill was again contemplating marriage. Muriel Wilson belonged to a grand and wealthy family, was considered one of Britain's most beautiful women, and was highly accomplished. She had a flair for amateur dramatics, and cut a dashing figure in costume. Churchill had known her for many years and his feelings had morphed from the friendly into the romantic. He proposed, and was once again disappointed.

Over the course of 1904 and 1905 Churchill wrote a number of impassioned letters to Wilson, two of which are reproduced below.

In the first, undated letter the sting of rejection is still palpable, as Churchill seeks desperately to persuade her to reconsider. However, his entreaties were to no avail. Wilson was fond of Churchill, but not romantically inclined towards him. Politics was of little interest to her, and she valued her independence too much to consider matrimony. It is evident from his letters that Churchill is attracted to her for her free-spiritedness; in contrast to the 'grey world of politics' she offers 'warmth' and 'glitter'. However, the pleasure she took in male company sometimes rankled; Churchill was particularly infuriated by her flirtation with the Portuguese ambassador, and notorious womaniser, Luis de Soveray. Writing to her in Cannes, the letter of 1905 barely conceals a note of jealous petulance as he denies all claims upon her and bids her 'career around Italy with anyone you choose'. Although the forays into personal news and political gossip imbue this letter with a certain light-heartedness, its lapse into 'growl[ing]' anger and despondency reveal that the wounds of the previous year have far from healed.

In 1906, Churchill was appointed to his first ministerial role in Balfour's new Liberal government, and progressed quickly to the cabinet. By the outbreak of the First World War he held a key position in the Admiralty Office. His private affairs also took an upturn during this period. Having been introduced to Clementine Hozier in 1904 (when he was still pining for Wilson) the pair met again in 1908 and were married later that year. The interwar years brought Churchill chequered political fortunes; periods of influence were interspersed with spells of exclusion from office. Although active in advising the government in the period leading up to the Second World War, it was not until the day that war was declared, 3 September 1939, that Chamberlain reinstated Churchill in his government as a member of the War

Cabinet. It was from this point that Churchill entered decisively upon the world stage, and the iconic figure of Britain's wartime leader was born.

∽

105, Mount Street, W.
[1904]

This is what I wanted to say on the way back – you are not certain in your own mind. Don't slam the door. I can wait – perhaps I shall improve with waiting. Why shouldn't you care about me someday? I have great faith in my instinct which was so very strong. Time and circumstances will work for me. Meanwhile I won't pester you. Let me see you again before Monday. I will try to talk banalities. At present I feel quite sick – and I will write and tell you when I have rearranged my mind and can see you without alluding to the only thing that is of the slightest consequence.

Of course if you don't care about me at all, you are quite right. But it is a sad pity & a scattering of treasure. I love you because you are good and beautiful, & you may be perfectly certain that I am not going to change or try to change. On the contrary the more I am opposed the more [tough] I shall feel – for I am not going to be thrust back into my grey world of politics without a struggle. But for that very reason you may see me safely – when I have got hold of myself again – for I won't be such a fool as to bore you …

Yours always –

Winston S. C.

Send me one line back.

∽

105, Mount Street, W.

7 September 1905

After all you are a friend. My letter was not really so rude as
it looked – because I never in my most secret heart make any
reproaches against you. I have absolutely no claim upon you.
You have never given me the smallest scrap of encouragement.
Indeed you have always been very kind to me. And if you
choose to career around Italy with anyone you chose – I should
have no right whatsoever to complain – even to myself. No
that is not what I have asked for. I have asked to be enabled
sometimes to see you – at my own risk – & I would gladly
bear any subsequent disappointment or sorrow that might – &
probably would come to me for the sake of the warmth and
glitter of your presence.

All this is very humble; but I am not humble really & growl
with anger to be treated with benevolent indifference. But what
can I do? It is a stupid world & I am a fool in it. Write to me as
you promise and tell me about your Italy … I shall look every
morning for that looped handwriting which sometimes disturbs
my letter bag so inconsequently …

I am concerned in an attempt to get Freddie into
parliament. He is clever & has just the kind of flashy gifts
which are a useful adjunct, if not a sufficient foundation for a
politician's reputation. If he gets in & Charlie Castlereagh too
we shall have quite a good polo team.

I have practically finished my book. You cannot think how
hard I have worked. Nearly 1100 pages of writing. But on the
whole I am satisfied. I think it will be a solid step. Did I tell you

that Longmans have offered me £4000 for it! I have replied. I want £6000 …

Have you followed the Curzon-Kitchener squabble? Of course I am a partisan of Curzon as representing the civil power against the military …

Harry Milner has accepted a most important office – v.i.z private secretary to Lord Derby. Everyone is astonished. But there is no accounting for tastes …

You will see by the fact that I am able to descend to gossip that I have somewhat composed & reorganised my mind. But … it was a struggle …

When you write to me – as I hope you will – do not neglect to put at the top of the first page your address in Florence & at Venice, so that I may write you some chatter back.

Yours always

Winston S. C.

P.S. That nice Barbara Lister – whom I used to like & admire so much – is married to a perfectly detestable nincompoop … His name is Wilson! I hope he is no relation of yours.

IRIS MURDOCH TO DAVID HICKS
AND RAYMOND QUENEAU

Iris Murdoch 1919–1999; David Hicks 1916–1991;
Raymond Queneau 1903–1976

'Love', writes Iris Murdoch in her journal, 'is, perhaps, the only subject on which I am expert.' This expertise derived not only from her academic interests but from her personal experience. The quest for love, selflessness and individual freedom proved a perennial topic of her philosophical and fictional works, while her private life overflowed with a plethora of passionate friendships, romantic attachments and sexual encounters.

While at Oxford in the late 1930s, Murdoch found herself 'quite astonishingly interested in the opposite sex' and the subject of widespread admiration. One young man particularly enamoured of her was Frank Thompson, with whom she maintained a close correspondence until his death during the Second World War. In 1942 she was conscripted to work at the Treasury. Her two years in London saw a series of messy romantic entanglements, including her relationships with future historian M.R.D. Foot and economist Thomas Balogh. In 1944 she began work with the United Nations Relief and Rehabilitation Administration, and was posted first to Brussels and then to Austria.

During the war years Murdoch corresponded with David Hicks, an Oxford contemporary with whom she had been briefly involved in 1938. Their letters became increasingly affectionate and in 1945, having spent ten days together in London, they became engaged. In a letter of December Iris excitedly anticipates 'the trials and high winds of our life together!' However, in February 1946 Hicks, now stationed in Czechoslovakia, writes to inform her that he has fallen in love with someone else. Murdoch's self-possessed letter, below, is written in response to this sudden retraction. Its measured, compassionate tone is only occasionally destabilised by a faint note of resentment, as when she refers to his new paramour as 'this Dornford Yates heroine' (a reference to a British novelist of the interwar years whose heroines were predictably uniform) and to a previous Iranian lover as 'old Muluk'.

Following a year in Cambridge as a postgraduate student Murdoch obtained a teaching post in philosophy at Oxford in 1948. During the 1950s her status as a philosopher, writer and public intellectual grew. Romantic interests included a host of London and Oxford academics including Wallace Robson, Michael Oakeshott and Franz Steiner and the author Elias Canetti. During this period she also maintained a correspondence with married French writer and artist Raymond Queneau, whom she had met in Innsbruck in 1946. At that time she had written to Queneau of her admiration for him 'as a supreme creator, and as yourself, Raymond', only to beat a hasty retreat in a subsequent letter: 'Please don't think that I "expect" anything of you – beyond, I hope, your continued friendship'. Yet Murdoch's feelings for Queneau far outstripped those of friendship. Her letter of August 1952, below, was written following one of their sporadic meetings in Paris and alludes to a 'scene' in which she disclosed her feelings for him. In the letter she expresses frankly her 'absolute' and 'unconditional' love for him.

In her correspondence with both Hicks and Queneau, Murdoch laments not knowing her love interests better. Following their engagement in 1946 she writes to Hicks that she is 'often frightened because I feel I don't know you', while her confessional letter to Queneau includes recognition of the 'distance' between them. In her philosophic thinking upon love, Murdoch is fascinated by the possibilities and limitations of knowing oneself and others; her understanding of morality includes a quest for interpersonal clear-sightedness. Yet she is, too, acutely conscious of the tensions, destructivity and potential madness that love can usher in. In a letter of 1964 she writes simply that 'When I am in love I am INSANE and although a great glory shines around, the main results are anxiety, misery, despair'. Her novels frequently navigate these murky backwaters of romance, as in the explorations of obsessional love in *The Sea, The Sea* and *The Black Prince*.

In 1956 Murdoch married English academic John Bayley, yet this did not put an end to her complicated and unconventional private life. The late 1950s and 1960s saw Murdoch engaged in a number of affairs with students and relationships with women. Throughout her life Murdoch maintained multiple, overlapping, intense relationships, and viewed friendship, love and sex as fluid affairs. Bayley, to whom she remained married until her death from Alzheimer's disease in 1999, described her passion for people thus: 'She fell in love all the time ... But she also fell into friendship all the time ... She lived literally for love and friendship.'

To David Hicks

UNRRA Central HQ, Vienna

18 February 1946

My dear, your letter of 21st January has just come. A shock, yes. It's hard to know what to say. It's frightening how people can deceive themselves and how quickly their moods can change, from very deep too. Yet it did seem stable, in spite of our panics. Thank you for having had the guts to write so frankly (even lyrically, if I may say so). What do I suggest? Well, I suggest we quietly call it off as far as you and I are concerned. There seems little choice – and in my saner moments I do see that it would have been risky. I don't seem to have a real gift for making you happy, and others have it, that's that. Further, I'd suggest that you *don't* marry this Dornford Yates heroine without considerable reflection and lapse of time. For heaven's sake don't tie yourself up in a moment of exaltation to someone you'll gradually find out to be not intelligent enough or profound enough for you. Remember that you've just nearly made one mistake – don't go and make another. Take it coolly and gently. If you do *so* much want to get married, why not consider old Muluk who *would* be faithful to you and *did* make you happy? I feel afraid for you, miserable in Bratislava and being pressed for decisions. Don't make them. Also, don't fret at all about me. I see the wisdom of our conclusion and I'm not shattered by it.

I hope you got my letters addressed to British Council of Bratislava – not that it matters, since letters from me must be simply an occasion of embarrassment now. You must have been miserable in this interval waiting for my answer. Well, darling don't be miserable any more. Concentrate on being *prudent*.

Do write to me please and tell me what's happening and be as frank as you can. And don't worry about me because I am perfectly all right and only wishing you not to be a fool and wreck your chances of happiness. You are a splendid creature David and lots of splendid women will want to marry you, so don't throw yourself away on someone unworthy.

I care very much about your being happy.

All my love, and write soon.

∽

To Raymond Queneau

[24 August 1952]

I'm sorry about the scene on the bridge – or rather, I'm sorry in the sense that I ought either to have said nothing or to have said something sooner. I was in extreme pain when I came to see you chez Gallimard on Friday – but what with English habitual reticence, and your cool way of keeping me at a distance I could say nothing although I wanted desperately to take you in my arms.

On the other hand, if I had started to talk sooner I might have spent the rest of the time (such as it was) in tears, and that was to be avoided. I'm glad I said at least one word to you however. I can't tell you what extravagances I have uttered in my heart and you have been spared. I write this now partly (for once) to relieve my feelings – and partly because you were (or affected to be??) surprised at what I said.

Listen – I love you in the most absolute sense possible. I would do anything for you, be anything you wished me, come to you at any time or place if you wished it even for a moment.

I should like to state this categorically since the moment for repeating it may not recur soon. If I thought I stood the faintest chance, *vis à vis de toi* [with you], I would fight and struggle savagely. As it is – there are not only the barriers between us of marriage, language, *La Manche* [the English Channel], and doubtless others – there is also the fact you don't need me in the way in which I need you – which is proved by the amount of time you are prepared to devote to me while I am in Paris. As far as I am concerned, this is *d'ailleurs* [anyway], an old story – when you said to me once, *recommençons un peu plus haut* [let's start again on a higher plane], it was already too late for me to do anything of the kind.

… I don't want to trouble you with this – or rather, not often! I know how painful it is to receive this sort of a letter, how one says to oneself oh my God! and turns over the page. I can certainly live without you – it's necessary, and what is necessary is possible, which is just as well. But what I write now expresses no momentary Parisian mood but simply where I stand. You know yourself what it is for one person to represent for another *an absolute* – and so you do for me. I don't think about you all the time. But I know that there is nothing I wouldn't give up for you if you wanted me. I'm glad to write this (*remember it*) in case you should ever feel in need of an absolute devotion …

Don't be distressed. To say these things takes a weight from my heart. The tone dictated to me by your letters *depuis des années me convient peu* [over the last few years hasn't answered my needs]. I don't know you quite well enough to know if this is *voulu* [deliberate] or not. Just as I wasn't sure about your 'surprise' on the bridge. To see you in this impersonal way in Paris, sitting in cafés and knowing you will be gone in an hour, is a *supplice* [torment]. But I well understand and am (I suppose) prepared to digest it, that there is no alternative …

… It's happened to me once, twice, perhaps three times in my life to feel an *unconditional* devotion to someone. The other recipients have gone on their way. You remain. There is no substitute for this sort of sentiment and no mistaking it when it occurs …

… I love you, I love you absolutely and unconditionally – thank God for being able to say this with the whole heart.

I feel reluctant to close this letter because I know I shan't feel so frank later on. Not that my feelings will have altered, *ça ne change pas* [they do not change], but I shall feel more acutely the futility of these sort of exclamations. At this moment I am, *même malgré toi* [even in spite of you], in communication with you in a way which may not be repeated.

… Forgive what in this letter is purely 'tiresome'. Accept what you can. If there is anything here which can give you pleasure or could in any bad moment give you comfort I should be very happy. I love you so deeply that I can't help feeling that it must 'touch' you somehow, even without your knowing it.

Again, don't be distressed. There is so much I should like to have said to you, and may one day. I don't want to stop writing – I feel I am leaving you again. My very very dear Queneau –

I

W.B. YEATS AND MAUD GONNE

William Butler Yeats 1865–1939; Maud Gonne 1866–1953

In his memoir, W.B. Yeats, perhaps the most lauded poet of the twentieth century, reflects upon the significance of his falling in love with Irish revolutionary Maud Gonne: this was, he writes, when 'the troubling of my life began'. Yeats and Gonne first met in 1889, when Gonne called upon the Yeats family at their London home. The scholarly, shy Yeats was captivated by this self-possessed and outspoken heiress. Gonne was beautiful – tall and strong-featured with dark, deep-set eyes; a beauty Yeats would celebrate in many of his poems. Having both spent much of their childhood in Ireland and feeling deeply connected to the land, they were attracted to one another through a shared enthusiasm for Irish national identity.

Visiting her in Ireland in 1891 Yeats proposed marriage to Gonne. He was rejected. Yet despite this their intimacy deepened. They went walking together on the peninsula of Howth Head, a place they both loved, and Gonne shared with Yeats a dream she had in which they were brother and sister. He was later to recall this trip in 'Cycles Ago', a poem redolent with his romantic disappointment:

My world was fallen and over, for your dark soft eyes on it
　　shone;
A thousand years it had waited and now it is gone, it is gone.

Between 1891 and 1901 Yeats proposed to Gonne at least four times, and each time she rejected him. Unbeknown to Yeats, during the early 1890s Gonne was romantically entangled with the French politician Lucien Millevoye, with whom she had a son who died in infancy and a daughter, Iseult. It was not until 1894 that Gonne shared with Yeats the details of her secret domestic life in France.

In the course of the 1890s Gonne was active in the cause of various social injustices, such as the eviction of tenants and the treatment of political prisoners, and campaigned for Irish nationalism upon the international stage. Yeats' poetry of this period drew upon Irish myth and folklore, and he was heavily involved in the rejuvenation of Irish theatre. He became a leading figure in the Irish Literary Revival, a movement committed to withstanding the cultural influence of English rule. Although often separated, Yeats and Gonne corresponded frequently, and continued to develop their shared interest in the occult. In 1898, in Dublin, Yeats told Gonne that he had dreamed of kissing her. Gonne shared a vision she had the same night: a spirit guide had joined their hands and pronounced that they were married. The notion of a 'spiritual marriage', as signified by her vision, took hold.

Yeats was shaken when, in 1903, he learnt of Gonne's engagement to Major John MacBride. Below is an extract from a draft letter, dated January 1903, in which Yeats seeks to persuade Gonne against the marriage. He expresses his fear that in marrying she will debase her own soul, and injure their cause – the national, cultural and spiritual freedom of the Irish people. Yeats appeals to their mystical union as a reminder of the task they have undertaken, and as a means of asserting his own position as her spiritual husband. In her reply of February, Gonne seeks to reassure him that their friendship will not be altered by her marriage. The wedding took place later that year, though she and MacBride separated acrimoniously in 1905.

Gonne's two letters from 1908, below, illustrate something of the nature of her and Yeats' unique spiritual relationship. In the letter of July she tells of visiting Yeats astrally, and reflects upon the intensity of this union which, though unmarked by the body, involved a 'melt[ing] into one another till we formed *one being*'. She returns to the question of spiritual versus physical love in the letter of December, although here a sense of struggle is evident in her resistance of 'bodily desire'. Whether Gonne's preoccupation with physicality reflects an increased intimacy between herself and Yeats around this time is a matter of speculation. In the letter of May 1909 she writes of her own 'renunciation', and longs that Yeats too can be free of 'suffering and temptation'.

Persisting over five decades, theirs was, according to Gonne, an essentially spiritual union. Yet Yeats repeatedly sought the more conventional bond of marriage. In 1916 he made one final proposal to Gonne and, with her permission, to her daughter Iseult, before finally marrying Georgina Hyde Lee in 1917. Although their friendship endured, Yeats and Gonne's politics diverged in the decades that followed: Yeats served in the Senate of the Irish Free State, while Gonne continued her activism. Yeats' won the Nobel Prize for Literature in 1923, and his literary success continued unabated until his death.

W.B. Yeats to Maud Gonne

[Late January 1903]

I appeal to you in the name of 14 years of friendship to read this letter. It is perhaps the last thing I shall write to you.

... I thought over things last night. The thought came to me 'you are not writing to her quite fully what you think. You fear to make her angry, to spoil her memory of you. Write all that you would have her know. Not to do so is mere selfishness. It is too late now to think of anything but the truth. If you do not speak no one will' ... Your hands were put in mine & we were told to do a certain great work together. For all who undertake such tasks there comes a moment of extreme peril. If you carry out your purpose you will fall into a lower order & do great injury to the religion of free souls that is growing up in Ireland, it may be to enlighten the whole world ... You possess your influence in Ireland very largely because you come to the people from above. You represent a superior class, a class whose people are more independent, have a more beautiful life, a refined life ... Maud Gonne is surrounded by romance. She puts away from her what seems an easy & splendid life that she may devote herself to the people ... But Maud Gonne is about to pass away ... you are going to marry one of the people ... thrusting you down to the people ... They will never forgive it ... now I appeal, I whose hands were placed in yours by eternal hands, to come back to yourself. To take up again the proud solitary haughty life which made you seem like one of the Golden Gods. Do not, you [who] seem the most strong, the most inspired be the first to betray us, to betray the truth ... [it] is not only the truth & your friends but your own soul that you are about to betray.

⤜⤚

Maud Gonne to W.B. Yeats

5 Rue de Paradis, Laval, Mayeune
10 February [1903]

My dear Friend

I have your three letters – they have made me sad, because I fear that you are sad & yet our friendship need not suffer by my marriage. You have known me for many years in the ups and downs of a rather agitated life, yet you have always found me the same as far as our friendship was concerned. So it will always be …

… You say I leave the few to mix myself with the crowd while Willie I have always told you I am the voice, the soul of the *crowd*.

… Friend of mine au revoir. I shall go over to Ireland in a couple of months, if you care to see me I shall be so glad & you will find I think I am just the same woman you have always known, marriage won't change me I think at all. I intend to keep my own name & to go on with all my work the same as ever …

Maud Gonne.

❦

Paris
26 July [1908]

Willie

… I had such a wonderful experience last night that I must know at once if it affected you & how? For above all I don't want to do anything which will take you from your work, or make working more arduous …

Last night all my household had retired at a quarter to 11 and I thought I would go to you astrally. It was not working hours for you & I thought by going to you I might even be able to leave with you some of my vitality & energy … I had seen the day before when waking from sleep a curious somewhat Egyptian form floating over me … It was dressed in moth like garments & had curious wings edged with gold in which it could fold itself up – I had thought it was myself, a body in which I could go out into the astral – at a quarter to 11 last night I … thought strongly of you & desired to go to you. We went somewhere in space I don't know where – I was conscious of starlight & of hearing the sea below us. You had taken the form I think of a great serpent, but I am not quite sure. I only saw your face distinctly & as I looked into your eyes (as I did the day in Paris you asked me what I was thinking of) & your lips touched mine. We melted into one another till we formed only *one being, a being greater than ourselves* who felt all & knew all with double intensity – the clock striking 11 broke the spell & as we separated it felt as if life was being drawn away from me through my chest with almost physical pain … Then I went upstairs to bed & I dreamed of you … We were quite happy, & we talked of this wonderful spiritual vision I have described – you said it would tend to increase physical desire – This troubles me a little – for there was nothing physical in that union – Material union is but a pale shadow compared to it – write to me quickly & tell me if you know anything of this & what you think of it – & if I may come to you again like this. I shall not until I hear from you. My thought with you always.

Maud Gonne.

〰

13 Rue de Passy, Paris
[December 1908]

Dearest

… You asked me yesterday if I am not a little sad that things are as they are between us – I am sorry & I am glad. It is hard being away from each other so much there are moments when I am dreadfully lonely & long to be with you, – one of these moments is on me now – but beloved I am glad & proud beyond measure of your love, & that it is strong enough and high enough to accept the spiritual love & union I offer –

I have prayed so hard to have all earthly desire taken from my love for you & dearest, loving you as I do, I have prayed & I am praying still that the bodily desire for me may be taken from you too. I know how hard & rare a thing it is for a man to hold spiritual love when the bodily desire is gone & I have not made these prayers without a terrible struggle a struggle that shook my life though I do not speak much of it & generally manage to laugh.

That struggle is over & I have found peace. I think today I could let you marry another without losing it – for I know the spiritual union between us will outlive this life, even if we never see each other in this world again.

Write to me soon.

Yours

Maud

〰

On the boat going to Ireland
[May 1909]

Beloved

… I have not come to the decision I have come to without struggle & without suffering … I will pray with my whole strength that suffering & temptation may be taken from you as they have from me & that we may gain spiritual union stronger than earthly union could ever be.

I want to thank you my own for being generous with me *as you have always been*. I have brought suffering to you so often, & you never reproach me. – Will I ever bring you happiness & peace to compensate? I pray to God that by holding our love pure it may be so.

… My loved one I belong to you more in this renunciation than if I came to you in sin. Did you not say yourself that our love must be holy?

Yours
Maud

ANDRE DE DIENES
TO MARILYN MONROE

Andre de Dienes 1913–1985; Marilyn Monroe 1926–1962

───────◦◦◦◦◦───────

Hungarian-American photographer Andre de Dienes first met
Norma Jeane Mortenson, soon to metamorphose into the
Hollywood star Marilyn Monroe, when she was an inexperienced
nineteen-year-old model. Living in New York in the early 1940s,
de Dienes enjoyed an international reputation as a talented fashion
photographer. Yet a desire to pursue his artistic interests in pho-
tographing nudes and the natural landscape drew him out west.
Arriving in California, he approached a modelling agency in search
of a muse, and recalls Norma Jeane's appearance on his doorstep
in June 1945: 'She was wearing a skimpy pink sweater, her curly
hair tied with a ribbon to match ... I immediately felt how much I
could draw out of her ... In one fell swoop I was intrigued, moved
and attracted by her.'

Their early shoots yielded a series of fresh, lively photographs
– of Norma Jeane barefoot upon a highway, perched upon a farm
gate, or sand-covered on a Malibu beach. Soon de Dienes arranged
for them to take a road trip together, motivated by joint professional and personal desires: he longed to capture her beauty in
a more dramatic setting and to initiate a romantic relationship.
This trip, which took them to the Mojave Desert and eventually to Portland, Oregon, bred intimacy. Following a number of
unsuccessful attempts at seduction, de Dienes' hopes were fulfilled

when, holed up in their hotel room by a snowstorm, the couple spent a languorous day making love.

Following this trip de Dienes planned to marry Norma Jeane as soon as possible. She, however, was not so inclined: she had her heart set on a career in the movies and was still extricating herself from her first marriage (entered into at the age of sixteen). Having temporarily moved back to New York, and impatient to speed matters along, de Dienes quit his job and returned to see Norma Jeane in California. He arranged to meet her, but she did not keep the appointment. He then went to her home and, finding her in a negligee and the bed disarrayed, realised he was not her only paramour. That evening he drove to the cliffs and contemplated suicide, but ended up shooting pictures of the sunset instead.

During the latter half of the 1940s Norma Jeane broke into the film industry and adopted her new name, Marilyn Monroe. Her fame rocketed over the course of the 1950s, and she gained the status of one of the most glamorous and sexually alluring actresses in Hollywood. Two further marriages – to baseball star Joe DiMaggio in 1954 and playwright Arthur Miller in 1956 – ended in divorce. Gradually her health, both mental and physical, declined. She suffered from gynaecological illness, experienced a number of failed pregnancies, and relied increasingly heavily upon barbiturates and alcohol to counter chronic insomnia and anxiety. She died of an overdose in 1962.

De Dienes pursued a highly successful photographic career and married twice. He took many more iconic images of Marilyn, and their relationship continued to be marked by moments of intimacy, dependence and occasional tempestuousness. This closeness is illustrated in de Dienes' letter from 1960, below. Here he complains of having read a biographical article on Marilyn in which he does not figure, yet his annoyance is tempered by the strange pet names with which he addresses her. De Dienes did not, it would seem, ever fully exorcise his fascination with Norma Jeane. In his memoir, only discovered after his death, he reflects on how their affair, 'brief and violent as a thunderstorm', left – like the impression of light upon a photographic film – 'its mark on me forever'.

∽

29 March 1960

Dear turkey foot:

I glanced through your biography in the April issue of Mccall's and as usual, I did not find my name somewhere where it should have been mentioned – after all, I was a turning point in your life I always believed, and you yourself know it very well.

But I am not surprised you never mention me, for years now you did that same thing – got even with me. I shall never forget the incident when one Sunday we were driving along and had a short dispute about something, and I told you angrily 'you will never be an actress' and you got out of the car at the next corner. Well, that's what did it I know, and perhaps other things.

I have no hard feeling toward you even if you never think of me, however I think it is a little bit funny that you did not mention all the lovely photos I took of you back in 45, 46, 47, 49, and so on.

Some day, when I will have time I shall write my memoirs also, and will be kinder than you are and will mention you in it.

I have always been a discreet person, did not want to make lots of hullaballoo about things – I was wrong I admit it – while you made such an enormous story about yourself – or rather – others did it for you.

Well, that's the way life goes sometimes.

Incidentally, I left a short letter to you at your hotel a few weeks ago, wanted to photograph you for a magazine. You had probably left already, or were bored to do it, or perhaps you thought those kind of lousy photos like I saw in Life magazine a week or so ago when the strike began at the Studio – will do you more good. Well, you looked pretty thin and old, and so did the other actors too in that layout. I was kind of peeved, how a great magazine like Life could send out a photographer to shoot such miserable looking photos.

Have to run now. Bless you, little mushroom – will see you some day – Am going up north this summer, through the redwoods, will think of you in the big forests.

Regards,

[Andre D]

HENRY VIII TO ANNE BOLEYN

Henry VIII 1491–1547; Anne Boleyn (c. 1501–07)–1536

Henry VIII is remembered as a wilful monarch, bent on satisfying his desires. Certainly he pursued one particular goal – his marriage to Anne Boleyn – with marked tenacity. By the time Anne arrived in court in 1522, Henry was already contemplating how best to extricate himself from his marriage to the ageing Katherine of Aragon. His infatuation with Anne compounded his determination to marry again, and hopefully sire his longed-for male heir. Ultimately he was prepared to break decisively with Papal authority and reconfigure the religious landscape of the nation in order to attain his desired end.

Having spent almost seven years serving as a lady-in-waiting to Queen Claude of France, Anne had been schooled in the manners of the French court. With her captivating dark eyes, Continental allure and elegance upon the dance floor, it was not long before she was enjoying the attention of numerous admirers. In 1523 Anne became engaged to one of her suitors, Henry Percy, yet Cardinal Wolsey intervened to break the engagement, possibly at the King's bidding. It was not until 1526, however, that Henry's passion for Anne was fully awakened and he asked her to become his mistress. Anne refused – reluctant, perhaps, to jeopardise her favoured position by succumbing too readily to the King's advances.

A series of love letters written from Henry to Anne chronicle the development of their romance. The letters included below are thought to have been written in early 1527, when Anne withdrew from court to her family home at Hever Castle. These letters indicate that Henry's passion initially outstripped that of Anne. In the first he speaks of his 'great agony' of uncertainty and, as a means of persuasion, promises Anne he will have no other mistress but her. The second letter suggests that her own correspondence was neither as frequent nor as fulsome as he would have liked. A keen huntsman, he sends her a buck he has killed as a reminder of his person. In the third letter Henry expresses his hope that their passion will be heightened by distance, yet the fourth refers ruefully to Anne's flightiness; having earlier agreed to attend court, it seems she has now retracted the decision, leaving Henry in a state of confusion. Although Anne was probably careful to withhold her full commitment at this stage, it is also worth remembering that Henry's complaints are penned in the spirit of courtly love; he casts himself in the role of a suffering 'servant' who idolises his wilful lady.

It was not until the late spring of 1527 that Anne accepted Henry's proposal of marriage, on the understanding that he was to seek an annulment from Katherine. As ecclesiastical investigations into the validity of his marriage began, Anne was little at court. She and the King spent time together at Hever, the Palace of Beaulieu, and Windsor Castle. The letters from this period tell of an increasing intimacy between the couple, although it is probable that Anne continued to withhold certain favours until her position beside Henry as wife, rather than mistress, was secured. On one occasion Henry wishes Anne 'in my arms', on another he desires to be 'at this moment privately with you'. Still more explicitly, he hopes soon to be able to kiss her 'pretty dukkys' (breasts), and indulges in some double-entendre when sending her a further hunting trophy: 'some flesh, representing my name [...] prognosticating that hereafter, God willing, you may enjoy some of mine'.

Anne was increasingly accorded a privileged position at court and was established in her own residence. Henry kept her continually close by and showered her with gifts. A turning point in the courtship came in 1532: Anne was elevated to the peerage; she accompanied Henry upon a diplomatic trip to Calais, and it seems likely that the relationship was finally consummated. They were married in a secret ceremony in London in January 1533. Following Cardinal Wolsey's unsuccessful attempts to gain an annulment from Rome, Henry's new chief adviser Thomas Cromwell embarked upon a course of parliamentary legislation to cut back upon Papal power. These political exigencies ultimately resulted in the establishment of the Church of England, and ushered in the English Reformation. In June Anne was crowned Queen in a lavish ceremony at Westminster Abbey, and in September their daughter Elizabeth (later to become Queen Elizabeth I) was born.

Yet this union, so hard-won, proved short-lived. The path that led Anne from her coronation to the Tower is paved with court intrigue (she was an unpopular Queen), Henry's growing impatience for a son (Anne suffered at least two miscarriages), Anne's own spirited character (leading her to quarrel with the King), and Henry's growing attraction to Jane Seymour. In 1536 Anne found herself imprisoned on charges of adultery, incest and conspiring against the King and, on 19 May, had her head cleanly dispatched by a French swordsman. Her husband – who had once written to her 'beseeching you to apprise me of your welfare, which I pray to God may continue as long as I desire mine own' – married again later that month.

⚮

[c. early 1527]

On turning over in my mind the contents of your last letters, I have put myself into great agony, not knowing how to interpret them, whether to my disadvantage, as you show in some places, or to my advantage, as I understand them in some others, beseeching you earnestly to let me know expressly your whole mind as to the love between us two. It is absolutely necessary for me to obtain this answer, having been for above a whole year stricken with the dart of love, and not yet sure whether I shall fail of finding a place in your heart and affection, which last point has prevented me for some time past from calling you my mistress; because, if you only love me with an ordinary love, that name is not suitable for you, because it denotes a singular love, which is far from common. But if you please to do the office of a true loyal mistress and friend, and to give up yourself body and heart to me, who will be, and have been, your most loyal servant, (if your rigour does not forbid me) I promise you that not only the name shall be given you, but also that I will take you for my only mistress, casting off all others besides you out of my thoughts and affections, and serve you only. I beseech you to give an entire answer to this my rude letter, that I may know on what and how far I may depend. And if it does not please you to answer me in writing, appoint some place where I may have it by word of mouth, and I will go thither with all my heart. No more, for fear of tiring you. Written by the hand of him who would willingly remain yours, H. R.

∾

[c. early 1527]

Although, my mistress, it has not pleased you to remember
the promise you made me when I was last with you – that is,
to hear good news from you, and to have an answer to my
last letter; yet it seems to me that it belongs to a true servant
(seeing that otherwise he can know nothing) to inquire the
health of his mistress, and to acquit myself of the duty of a true
servant, I send you this letter, beseeching you to apprise me
of your welfare, which I pray to God may continue as long as
I desire mine own. And to cause you yet oftener to remember
me, I send you, by the bearer of this, a buck killed late last
night by my own hand, hoping that when you eat of it you may
think of the hunter …

∾

[c. early 1527]

My Mistress & Friend, my heart and I surrender ourselves
into your hands, beseeching you to hold us commended to your
favour, and that by absence your affection to us may not be
lessened: for it were a great pity to increase our pain, of which
absence produces enough and more than I could ever have
thought could be felt, reminding us of a point in astronomy
which is this: the longer the days are, the more distant is the
sun, and nevertheless the hotter; so is it with our love, for
by absence we are kept a distance from one another, and yet
it retains its fervour, at least on my side; I hope the like on
yours …

⌇

[c. early 1527]

To my mistress. Because the time seems very long since I heard concerning your health and you, the great affection I have for you has induced me to send you this bearer, to be better informed of your health and pleasure, and because, since my parting from you, I have been told that the opinion in which I left you is totally changed, and that you would not come to court either with your mother, if you could, or in any other manner; which report, if true, I cannot sufficiently marvel at, because I am sure that I have since never done any thing to offend you, and it seems a very poor return for the great love which I bear you to keep me at a distance both from the speech and the person of the woman that I esteem most in the world: and if you love me with as much affection as I hope you do, I am sure that the distance of our two persons would be a little irksome to you, though this does not belong so much to the mistress as to the servant.

Consider well, my mistress, that absence from you grieves me sorely, hoping that it is not your will that it should be so; but if I knew for certain that you voluntarily desired it, I could do no other than mourn my ill-fortune, and by degrees abate my great folly. And so, for lack of time, I make an end of this rude letter, beseeching you to give credence to this bearer in all that he will tell you from me.

Written by the hand of your entire Servant,

H. R.

VIRGINIA STEPHEN
AND LEONARD WOOLF

Virginia Woolf (née Stephen) 1882–1941;
Leonard Woolf 1880–1969

———◦◦◦———

In Virginia Woolf's first novel, *The Voyage Out*, Rachel muses on her forthcoming marriage to Terence: 'although she was going to marry him and to live with him … and to quarrel, and to be so close to him, she was independent of him'. What sort of marriage is desirable? And how is one to balance the closeness of marriage with the separateness of two individuals? Such questions ripple through Woolf's fiction, as they did through her own romantic life.

Leonard Woolf was at Cambridge with Virginia's brother, Thoby. On the occasions that he met the Stephen sisters, Virginia and Vanessa, he was impressed by their beauty. In 1904 Leonard embarked on a career with the Colonial Service in Ceylon. He was abroad for more than six years, during which time his friend Lytton Strachey encouraged him to consider Virginia as a potential wife. Virginia was by this time living in London with her sister, hosting regular soirees of artists and writers – a set that came to be known as the Bloomsbury group. Leonard returned to Britain on leave in 1911 and during the autumn and winter he and Virginia spent an increasing amount of time together.

On 11 January 1912 Leonard travelled from a friend's house in Somerset to propose to Virginia. Returning to Somerset that evening, his proposal as yet unanswered, he writes to Virginia of the 'hopeless uncertainty' that has plagued him up to that point. Virginia responds that she needs time to consider, and that she must remain 'honest'. In a breathless letter of 29 April, below, Leonard tells of his overwhelming love for Virginia, his inferiority to her, his confidence in the life they could have together, and his desire not to pressure her. In her reply of 1 May, also below, Virginia outlines various facets of her anxiety: suspicions over her own motives, a disinclination towards physical love, his Jewishness, her mental instability and, above all, a basic uncertainty that any individual can ever know another. Yet, as the letter continues, it is clear that the prospect of what their marriage could be – not conventional, but somehow more vehement and vibrant – holds great appeal. Leonard derived enough encouragement from this letter to resign from the Colonial Service.

Leonard's patience paid off. Virginia did come to love him, and they married on 10 August 1912. The early years of their marriage were blighted by Virginia's ill health. She had experienced mental breakdown before, and would continue to do so episodically throughout her life. She came to recognise, with fear, the tell-tale signs: 'I feel unreason slowly tingling in my veins'. Leonard took great pains to care for Virginia. He sought medical opinions and arranged their life so as best to ensure Virginia's health and safeguard her creativity. As part of this endeavour the couple split their time between London and the Sussex countryside they both loved.

There were some disappointments in their married life. As suggested by the courtship letters, Virginia desired children, yet on medical advice and for the sake of Virginia's health she and Leonard did not become parents. So too, Virginia's distaste for sex, hinted at in her letter of May 1912, persisted. Nonetheless, the Woolfs' marriage was one of great intimacy and affection. In June 1925 Virginia writes in her diary that it is the most commonplace aspects of her and Leonard's life that make it an 'immense success' – the enjoyment they derive from a bus ride, or sitting down after dinner. In an entry of 1937 she notes simply that it is 'an enormous pleasure, being wanted: a wife'.

Despite her periods of illness, Virginia remained highly productive throughout her life. Through her lyrical, fluid narratives she conveys the modulating landscape of inner experience and the incomplete quality of perception. Her experimental prose secured her reputation as one of the foremost modernist writers of the twentieth century. In addition to her novels, she also wrote short stories, biographies and critical works, and reviewed for the *Times Literary Supplement*. Leonard, meanwhile, pursued a multifaceted career: he wrote short stories and two novels, worked in publishing (with the Hogarth Press, which he and Virginia had founded in 1917), and was active in the realm of politics and social reform.

In their home in Sussex, four miles from the English Channel, the Woolfs felt acutely the threat posed by Nazi Germany in the early days of the Second World War. This anxiety was, however, just one component of Virginia's slide towards suicide in 1941. She was suffering under the strain of her work and the old signs of breakdown were there: she was terrified by the sense of impending madness. On 28 March Virginia walked to the River Ouse, filled her pockets with stones, and waded into the water. In a note to Leonard she assures him of her joy in having married him: 'I want to tell you that you have given me complete happiness.'

Leonard to Virginia

[38 Brunswick Square]
29 April 1912

Dearest Virginia, I can't sleep not from desire but from thinking about you. I've been to the opera but for all that I heard of it I might have been sitting in this room. I've read two of your MSs [manuscripts] from one of which at any rate one can see that you might write something astonishingly good. I want to see you to talk with you & now, though I suppose I shouldn't, I'm going to write utterly miserable what I should want to say to you & probably couldn't.

Since yesterday something seemed to rise up in you against me. It may be imagination on my part; if it is, you must forgive me: I don't think even you realise what it would mean to me. God, the happiness I've had by being with you & talking with you as I've sometimes felt it mind to mind together & soul to soul. I know clearly enough what I feel for you. It is not only physical love though it is that of course & I count it the least part of it, it isn't only that I'm only happy with you, that I want to live with you; it's that I want your love too. It's true that I'm cold & reserved to other people; I don't feel affection ever easily: but apart from love I'm fond of you as I've never been of anyone or thing in the world. We often laugh about your lovableness but you don't know how lovable you are. It's what really keeps me awake far more than any desire. It's what worries me now, tears me two ways sometimes – for I wouldn't have you marry me, much as I love you, if I thought that it would bring you any unhappiness. Really this is true though it hurt me more than the worst physical pain your mere words that you told Vanessa that probably you would never marry anyone.

There is nothing that you've done which hasn't seemed
to me absolutely right which hasn't made me love you more.
I've never for a single moment thought you were treating me
badly & I never shall, whether you marry me or not. I love you
more for not deciding – I know the reasons. You are far finer,
nobler, better than I am. It isn't difficult to be in love with you
& when one is in love with anyone like you one has to make no
allowances, no reservations. But I've many beastly qualities –
though I've shown them to you deliberately often because I'm
too fond of you not to want you to know that they do exist. For
me to know that they do exist & to be in love with someone like
you, that's where the pain comes in.

I don't want you to decide until you've finished your novel,
I think you're right not to. I can go on as we've been doing for
six months even, if you want it, or if you ever for a moment
feel it would be easier, I will go away for a week or a month or
longer – though not seeing you for a day makes me miserable
now. But I believe I know how you feel now & one should
speak out what one thinks. I should like to say it to you, only
when I'm with you all sorts of feelings make it so difficult to
say exactly what I mean – so that it's a good thing perhaps that
I am writing to you. I believe you might very easily be in love
now & almost equally easily never be – with me at any rate. I
don't think much of the physical part of it though it must come
in – but it's so elusive. If one happens to be born as I am, it
is almost certain to be very strong, but even then it becomes
so merged with one's other feelings. It was the least strong of
my feelings for you when I fell in love & when I told you. It
has grown far more violent as my other feelings have grown
stronger.

I think we're reaching a point at which everything will tremble in the balance. Sometimes I suppose you don't know exactly what you feel & really unimportant things become magnified. I have faults, vices, beastlinesses but even with them I do believe you ought to marry me & be in love – & it isn't only because so often I feel that if you never are, the best thing in life will have gone. I shall never be like you, never anything like it, but you seem to purge my faults from me. And I have the fire in me at any rate & the knowledge. I want to live & get the best things in life & so do you. You are the best thing in life & to live it with you would make it ten thousand times more worth living. I shall never be content now with the second best. And you, I'm sure, you see that if it could be lived like that by two people who know how to live – God, the chance of it is worth any risk almost.

Virginia, I don't know where I've got to. I'm just writing as I think. It's nearly 3 in the morning. I shall go for a walk & post this & then go to bed again. I only hope there's nothing in it to worry you. At any rate you must know that I love you as much as it is possible for one human being to love another. I would rather do anything than harm you in the slightest possible way. You mustn't worry or hurry – there's no need for it. You must finish your novel first & while you are doing it you must not try to decide. If you don't try to decide & we go on as we have been, I shall get plenty of happiness in the next two months. After all I've had more happiness in the last two months than in all the rest of my life put together.

And writing like this to you is like talking to you, it makes all depression go. I shall go to bed happy & sleep peacefully. I hope you are.

L.

∽

Virginia to Leonard

Asheham [Rodmell, Sussex]
1 May [1912]

Dearest Leonard,

To deal with the facts first (my fingers are so cold I can hardly write) I shall be back about 7 tomorrow, so there will be time to discuss ...

Well then, as to all the rest. It seems to me that I am giving you a great deal of pain—some in the most casual way— and therefore I ought to be as plain with you as I can, because half the time I suspect, you're in a fog which I don't see at all. Of course I can't explain what I feel—these are some of the things that strike me. The obvious advantages of marriage stand in my way. I say to myself Anyhow, you'll be quite happy with him; and he will give you companionship, children, and a busy life—then I say By God, I will not look upon marriage as a profession. The only people who know of it, all think it suitable; and that makes me scrutinise my own motives all the more. Then, of course, I feel angry sometimes at the strength of your desire. Possibly, your being a Jew comes in also at this point. You seem so foreign. And then I am fearfully unstable. I pass from hot to cold in an instant, without any reason; except that I believe sheer physical effort and exhaustion influence me. All I can say is that in spite of these feelings which go chasing each other all day long when I am with you, there is some feeling which is permanent, and growing. You want to know of course whether it will ever make me marry you. How can I say? I think it will, because there seems no reason why it shouldn't — But I don't know what the future will bring. I'm half afraid of myself. I sometimes feel that no one ever has or ever can share something — It's the thing that makes you call me like a hill, or a rock. Again, I want everything — love, children, adventure, intimacy, work. (Can you make any sense out of this ramble? I am putting down one thing after another.) So I go from being half in love with you, and wanting you to be with me always, and know everything about me, to the extreme of wildness and aloofness. I sometimes think that if I married you, I could have everything — and then — is it the sexual side of it that comes between us? As I told you brutally the other day, I feel no physical attraction in you. There are moments — when you kissed me the other day was one — when I feel no more than a rock. And yet your caring for me as you do almost overwhelms me. It is so real, and so strange. Why should you? What am I really except a pleasant attractive creature? But it's just because you care so much that I feel I've got to care before I marry you. I feel I must give you everything; and that if I can't, well, marriage would only be second-best for you as well as for me. If you can still go on, as before, letting me find my own way, as that is what would please me best; and then we must both take the risks. But you have made me very happy too. We both of us want a marriage that is a tremendous living thing, always alive, always hot, not dead and easy in parts as most marriages are. We ask a great deal of life, don't we? Perhaps we shall get it; then, how splendid!

...Yrs.

VS

DAVID HUME TO
LA COMTESSE DE BOUFFLERS

David Hume 1711–1776; La Comtesse de Boufflers
(née Marie-Charlotte Hippolyte de Campet de Saujon) 1724–1800

———— ∞⊙∞ ————

David Hume was one of the most notable philosophers of the eighteenth century, and a leading light in the intellectual out-pouring known as the Scottish Enlightenment. Marked by a profound scepticism regarding the foundations of knowledge, Hume's thinking had a lasting impact upon political theory and economics as well as various branches of philosophy. In his life-time Hume was, however, best known for his six-volume *History of England*. It was in praise of this colossus that the French society hostess La Comtesse (countess) de Boufflers, the estranged wife of Le Comte de Boufflers and mistress of the Prince de Conti, wrote to the bachelor scholar in 1761. The work, she effuses, must have been written by 'some celestial being, free from human passions'. The years that followed put paid to such an assumption. In both his life and his philosophy Hume was alive to the strength of the passions; 'reason is,' he maintained, 'and ought only to be the slave of the passions.'

In 1763 Hume moved to Paris as undersecretary to the British ambassador Lord Hertford. He spent two sublimely happy years there. French intellectual society embraced him; he was lavished with praise and welcomed into the city's salons. These institutions, hosted by noblewomen, brought together an international array of intellectuals in pursuit of the furtherance of knowledge. One of the most opulent of these salons was that of La Comtesse de Boufflers, held in her grand townhouse in the enclos du Temple in the 3rd arrondissement. Following their correspondence, a close friendship was established between Hume and the Comtesse, and they spent much time in one another's company. Hume became besotted with his beautiful and urbane companion, and grew increasingly jealous of her affair with de Conti. Any hopes Hume may have nurtured of a lasting amour were likely dashed following the death of the Comtesse's husband in 1764, when her determination to marry the Prince de Conti became apparent.

In the letters below, dating from spring 1766, Hume's attachment is still very much in evidence. Following his return to Britain earlier that year, he longs for the Comtesse's company and laments that he ever left Paris. In the letter of April he refers enthusiastically to plans, aided by the Prince de Conti, to accommodate him in the du Temple area, while in the letter of May he indulges in the possibility that she may join him on a trip to Greece. He writes, too, at some length of Jean-Jacques Rousseau, for it was at the bidding of the Comtesse that Hume sought to assist the exiled French philosopher. It is likely that throughout their acquaintance Hume placed more store upon their intimacy than did the Comtesse: she was a woman practised in the art of flattery and flirtation, while Hume was by his own admission little versed in 'the pleasurable scenes of life'. Nonetheless, they continued corresponding until Hume's death, and it was with a lasting 'affection and regard' that he closed his final letter to the woman who had so excited his passions and tested his slavish reason.

Lisle Street, Leicester Fields
3 April 1766

It is impossible for me, dear Madam, to express the difficulty which I have to bear your absence, and the continual want which I feel of your society. I had accustomed myself of a long time, to think of you as a friend from whom I was never to be separated during any considerable time; and I had flattered myself that we were peculiarly fitted to pass our lives in intimacy and cordiality with each other. Age and a natural equability of temper were in danger of reducing my heart to too great indifference about every thing: it was enlivened by the charms of your conversation, and the vivacity of your character. Your mind, more agitated both by unhappy circumstances in your situation and by your natural disposition, could repose itself in the more calm sympathy which you found with me. But behold! Three months are elapsed since I left you; and it is impossible for me to assign a time when I can hope to join you. Lord Hertford has wrote me, that he expects to quit Ireland in a few weeks, and that he hopes to find me in London. I know that he proposed to be in France this summer; and he may probably desire me to delay my journey, that we may go together. I still return to my wish, that I had never left Paris, and that I had kept out of reach of all other duties, except that which was so sweet and agreeable to fulfil, the cultivating your friendship and enjoying your society. Your obliging expressions revive this regret in the strongest degree; especially where you mention the wounds which, though skinned over, still fester at the bottom.

Oh, my dear friend, how I dread that it may still be long ere you reach a state of tranquillity, in a distress which so

little admits of any remedy, and which the natural elevation
of your character, instead of putting you above it, makes you
feel with greater sensibility. I could only wish to administer the
temporary consolation, which the presence of a friend never
fails to afford.

The chief circumstance which hinders me from repenting of
my journey, is the use I have been to poor Rousseau, the most
singular, and often the most amiable man in the world.

I have now settled him in a manner entirely to my
satisfaction, and to his own. There is one Mr Davenport ...
Among several country seats which belong to him, he has
one in the county of Derby ... As he seldom lives there, he
proposed to me to give an apartment to our friend ...

I must confess, that I have not the consolation to think
he will long be happy there. Never was a man, who so well
deserves happiness, so little calculated by nature to attain it.
The extreme sensibility of his character is one great cause; but
still more, the frequent and violent fits of spleen and discontent
and impatience, to which, either from the constitution of his
mind or body, he is so subject ... When his health and good-
humour return, his lively imagination gives him so much
entertainment, that company, by disturbing his musing and
meditation, is rather troublesome to him; so that, in either case,
he is not framed for society ... He is commonly however the
best company in the world, when he will submit to live with
men ...

... I am at a loss in what terms to express my
acknowledgments to the Prince of Conti. Nothing can be more
honourable as well as agreeable to me, than the offer which he
is pleased to make me. I leave you to judge what addition the

pleasure of living in your company must make to all the other inviting circumstances that attend it. But there is only one particular which we must weigh together, when we meet.

When I return to Paris, it will be necessary for me to lay a plan of life more conformable to my character and usual habits: I must resolve to pass a great part of time among my books, and in retreat. How far will such a plan be consistent with the situation projected?

... I kiss your hands, with all the devotion possible.

∾

Lisle Street, Leicester Fields
16 May 1766

Nothing could have given me more pleasure than your letter. Though I never doubted your friendship, every instance of it affords me new satisfaction; especially one which opens to me the prospect of passing most of my time in your company. I could not wish for a more happy situation, nor one more conformable to my inclination. The objections appear to me, at this distance, very light in comparison of the advantages. But I reserve the forming of full judgement till our next meeting, which, I hope, will be after your return from Pougues.

...

... I have a project of accompanying you to Lyons. Would to God it were possible for us to take our flight thence into Italy; and from thence, if you would, into Greece. A friend of mine, who has been long settled in Smyrna, returns thither next spring, and urges me to take the journey along with him. What do you think of the project? The idea of it is not altogether extravagant. Might we not settle in some Greek island, and breathe the air of Homer or Sappho, or Anacreon, in tranquillity and great opulence? And might we not carry thither our philosopher of Derby, who will surely prefer that sunny situation to the mountains and clouds of this northern climate? Perhaps Madame de Bussy might consent to be of the party. Please remember to me that lady's situation, which is not indifferent to me, both on her own account, and on account of the interest you take in it. I kiss your hands, with great regard and attachment.

CHARLES DICKENS
TO MARIA BEADNELL

Charles Dickens 1812–1870; Maria Beadnell 1810–1886

'I don't remember who was there, except Dora. I have not the least idea what we had for dinner besides Dora … She had the most delightful little voice, the gayest little laugh, the pleasantest and most fascinating little ways, that ever led a lost youth into hopeless slavery.' It is thus that David Copperfield, hero of Dickens' novel of the same name, recalls meeting his first love. Charles Dickens was himself no stranger to the state of infatuation that he inflicts upon his protagonist. The novel's depiction of the youthful relationship between David and Dora has, at its heart, an experience from Dickens' own life.

In 1830, aged eighteen, Charles Dickens was working as a court reporter in the City of London. Having become acquainted with the Beadnell family, he was soon captivated by the girlish manner, dainty dress and harp-playing of the youngest daughter, Maria. Utterly enamoured, he penned some of his earliest writings, a number of sentimental love poems, in her honour. Yet he was aware of a social disparity between her family and his (her father was a senior bank clerk, while his own had been imprisoned for debt) and sought to better himself by pursuing a career in journalism. Nonetheless, Maria's parents did not consider him a suitable match. Initially Maria encouraged Dickens' attentions, and the couple corresponded secretly. Yet by 1833, following a period away at a finishing school in France, Maria's sentiments had cooled.

The first two letters below date from the troubled period of their relationship in the spring of 1833. In the letter of March, Dickens acknowledges the futility of his efforts to woo Maria. The letter, though well-mannered, reveals a cutting critique of her conduct. He implies that she has trifled with his emotions, offering him encouragement so as to maintain the interest of other suitors. A particular misunderstanding arose between them during this time: Maria accused Dickens of confiding too freely in her friend Mary Anne Leigh. In a series of letters Dickens seeks to defend himself against this charge, yet by the time he writes on 19 May he is clearly weary of the constant struggle for Maria's affections. He reiterates his love, yet leaves the question of their future in her hands. The relationship was to end soon after.

Over twenty years later Maria, now married and a mother of two, unexpectedly rekindled their correspondence. Dickens' letters of February 1855 reveal just how precious was the memory of his youthful passion, a 'perpetual idea' that he incubated over the ensuing years of literary success, fatherhood and a faltering marriage. It was thus with great disappointment that, upon dining with Maria and her husband, he realised that the qualities that had so charmed him in the young woman had become dull and irksome in middle age. Having immortalised her earlier self in the figure of Dora, Dickens proceeded to capture something of the older Maria in the comic character of Flora in *Little Dorrit*: 'Flora, who had been spoiled and artless long ago, was determined to be spoiled and artless now. That was a fatal blow.'

18 Bentinck Street
18 March [1833]

Dear Miss Beadnell,

Your own feelings will enable you to imagine far better than
any attempt of mine to describe the painful struggle it has
cost me to make up my mind to adopt the course which I now
take – a course than which nothing can be so directly opposed
to my wishes and feelings, but the necessity of which becomes
daily more apparent to me. Our meetings of late have been
little more than so many displays of heartless indifference
on the one hand, while on the other they have never failed
to prove a fertile source of wretchedness and misery; and
seeing, as I cannot fail to do, that I have engaged in a pursuit
which has long since been worse than hopeless and a further
perseverance in which can only expose me to deserved
ridicule, I have made up my mind to return the little present
I received from you some time since (which I have always
prized, as I still do, far beyond anything I ever possessed)
and the other enclosed mementos of our past correspondence
which I am sure it must be gratifying to you to receive, as
after our recent situations they are certainly better adapted
for your custody than mine.

Need I say that I have not the most remote idea of hurting
your feelings by the few lines which I think it necessary to
write with the accompanying little parcel? I must be the last
person in the world who could entertain such an intention,
but I feel that this is neither a matter nor a time for cold,
deliberate, calculating trifling. *My* feelings upon any subject,
more especially upon this, must be to you a matter of very
little moment; still I *have* feelings in common with other

people – perhaps so far as they relate to you they have been as strong and as good as ever warmed a human heart – and I do feel that it is mean and contemptible of me to keep by me one gift of yours or to preserve one single line or word of remembrance, or affection from you. I therefore return them, and I can only wish that I could as easily forget that I ever received them.

I have but one more word to say and I say it in my own vindication. The result of our past acquaintance is indeed a melancholy one to me. I have felt too long ever to lose the feeling of utter desolation and wretchedness which has succeeded our former acquaintance. Thank God I can claim for myself and *feel* that I deserve the merit of having ever throughout our intercourse acted fairly, intelligibly and honourably, under kindness and encouragement one day and a total change of conduct the next I have ever been the same. I have ever acted without reserve. I have never held out encouragement which I knew I never meant; I have never indirectly sanctioned hopes which I well knew I did not intend to fulfil. I have never made a mock confidante to whom to entrust a garbled story for my own purposes, and I think I never should (though God knows I am not likely to have the opportunity) encourage one danger as a useful shield for – an excellent set off against – others more fortunate and doubtless more deserving. I have done nothing that I could say would be very likely to hurt you … A wish for your happiness altho' it comes from me may not be the worse for being sincere and heartfelt. Accept it as it is meant, and believe that nothing will ever afford me more real delight than to hear that you, the object of my first and my last love, are happy. If you are happy

as I hope you may be, you will indeed possess every blessing
that this world can afford.

    C. D.

18 Bentinck Street

[19 May 1833]

Dear Miss Beadnell,

... I will only openly and at once say there is nothing I have
more at heart, nothing I more sincerely and earnestly desire,
than to be reconciled to you. It would be useless for me to
repeat here what I have so often said before; it would be
equally useless to look forward and state my hopes for the
future – all that anyone can do to raise himself to his exertions
and unceasing assiduity I have done, and will do. I have no
guide by which to ascertain your present feelings and I have,
God knows, no means of influencing them in my favour. I
never have loved and I can never love any human creature
breathing but yourself. We have had many differences, and
we have lately been entirely separated. Absence, however,
has not altered my feelings in the slightest degree, and the
Love I now tender you is as pure and as lasting as at any
period of our former correspondence. I have now done all I
can to remove our most unfortunate and to me most unhappy
misunderstanding. The matter now of course rests solely with
you, and you will decide as your own feelings and wishes
direct you. I could say much for myself and I could entreat a
favourable consideration on my own behalf but I purposely
abstain from doing so because it would be only a repetition

of an oft told tale and because I am sure that nothing I could say would have the effect of influencing your decision in any degree whatever …

Yours sincerely,
Charles Dickens.

∽

Tavistock House
10 February 1855

My Dear Mrs. Winter,
… I have been much moved by your letter; and the pleasure it has given me has some little sorrowful ingredient in it. In the strife and struggle of this great world where most of us lose each other so strangely, it is impossible to be spoken to out of the old times without a softened emotion. You so belong to the days when the qualities that have done me most good since, were growing in my boyish heart that I cannot end my answer to you lightly … We are all sailing away to the sea, and have a pleasure in thinking of the river we are upon, when it was very narrow and little.

Faithfully your friend,
Charles Dickens.

∽

Hotel Meurice, Paris
15 February 1855

My dear Mrs. Winter,

… I have always believed since, and always shall to the last, that there never was such a faithful and devoted poor fellow as I was. Whatever of fancy, romance, energy, passion, aspiration and determination belong to me, I never have separated and never shall separate from the hard-hearted little woman – you – whom it is nothing to say I would have died for, with the greatest alacrity! … It is a matter of perfect certainty to me that I began to fight my way out of poverty and obscurity, with one perpetual idea of you. This is so fixed in my knowledge that to the hour when I opened your letter last Friday night I have never heard anybody addressed by your name, or spoken of by your name, without a start. The sound of it has always filled me with a kind of pity and respect for the deep truth that I had, in my silly hobbledehoyhood, to bestow upon one creature who represented the whole world to me. I have never been so good a man since, as I was when you made me wretchedly happy. I shall never be half so good a fellow any more.

This is all so strange now both to think of, and to say, after every change that has come about; but I think, when you ask me to write to you, you are not unprepared for what it is so natural to me to recall, and will not be displeased to read it. I fancy – though you may not have thought in the old time how manfully I loved you – that you may have seen in one of my books a faithful reflection of the passion I had for you, and may have thought that it was something to have been loved so well, and may have seen in little bits of 'Dora' touches of your old self sometimes and a grace here and there that may be revived in your little girl's years hence, for the bewilderment of some other young lover – though he will never be as terribly in earnest as I and David Copperfield were. People used to say to me how pretty all that was, and how fanciful it was, and how elevated it was above the little foolish loves of very young men and women. But they little thought what reason I had to know it was true and nothing more nor less …

My Dear Mrs. Winter,
Ever affectionately yours,
Charles Dickens

CLAIRE CLAIRMONT
TO LORD BYRON

Claire Clairmont 1798–1879;
Lord George Gordon Byron 1788–1824

—∘⤜⤛∘—

A dalliance with the notoriously roguish Lord Byron brought her, Claire Clairmont was to claim in later life, a few moments of happiness and a lifetime of strife. Yet as a young woman Claire had found the allure of political radicalism, unbounded creativity and free love – as embodied in the lives of the romantic poets – impossible to resist.

Claire, christened Clara Mary Jane, was born illegitimately. Her mother married the widowed writer and political philosopher William Godwin when Claire was three. Of her two stepsisters (daughters of Godwin and proponent of women's rights Mary Wollstonecraft), Claire was particularly close to the younger, Mary. Claire abetted the clandestine romance which developed between Mary and poet Percy Bysshe Shelley, and accompanied the couple when they ran away together in 1814. As the three young libertines meandered their way through France and Switzerland, they immersed themselves in reading and writing, discussion and storytelling.

On their return to England, the trio maintained their unconventional living arrangements; Claire resided with the couple and was supported by Shelley. In 1816, in the hope of forging a career as a writer or actress, Claire began writing to George Gordon

Byron, a lauded poet and director of the Drury Lane Theatre. Yet her letters of this time, two examples of which are reproduced below, reveal a longing for more than professional mentorship: in one she declares her love for Byron, and in another instigates a secret rendezvous at an inn outside of town. Taking to heart Shelley's belief in the right of a woman to choose her lover, Claire instigates a sexual relationship with this man who, in her own words, 'once seen' was 'not to be forgotten'.

1816 was a difficult year for Byron. His marriage of the previous year, to Annabella Millbanke, crumbled. This provoked a scandal around his promiscuity and, in particular, the suspected incestuous relationship with his stepsister, Augusta Leigh. Dogged by debt and sickened by this furore, Byron left England in the summer of 1816. Although Byron responded to Claire's advances, he was in no way emotionally committed. In a letter to a friend he explains the extent of his interest in this 'odd-headed girl': 'I never loved her nor pretended to love her – but a man is a man – & if a girl of eighteen comes prancing to you at all hours of the night – there is but one way.'

Not easily deterred, Claire persuaded Mary and Shelley to follow Byron to Switzerland. She did not receive a warm welcome, with Byron refusing to be alone in her company. In the course of this visit it became apparent that Claire was pregnant. Claire and her companions returned to England at the end of the summer and Claire gave birth to a daughter, Allegra, early in 1817. Although he continued stalwart in his refusal to see Claire, Byron (now living in Italy) agreed to take in and raise their child. In the third letter below Claire pleads for more regular visits with Allegra and vigorously seeks to dissuade Byron from placing her in a convent. Claire's remonstrations remained unheeded, and it was with much bitterness as well as grief that she learnt of Allegra's death, aged five.

Over the course of the following fifty years Claire travelled widely, working as a governess, music teacher, companion and housekeeper. She finally settled in Florence, where she lived for almost a decade until her death in 1879. It was during her more peaceful final years that Claire penned her vitriolic memoir, in which she portrays the monstrousness of the liberated, romantic lifestyle for which she had once yearned.

∽

[1816]

An utter stranger takes the liberty of addressing you. It is earnestly requested that for one moment you pardon the intrusion, and, laying aside every circumstance of who and what you are, listen with a friendly ear … It is not charity I demand, for of that I stand in no need: I imply by that you should think kindly and gently of this letter, that if I seem impertinent you should pardon it for a while, and that you should wait patiently till I am emboldened by you to disclose myself.

I tremble with fear at the fate of this letter. I cannot blame if it shall be received by you as an impudent imposture. There are cases where virtue may stoop to assume the garb of folly; it is for the piercing eye of genius to discover her disguise, do you then give me credit for something better than this letter may seem to portend. Mine is a delicate case; my feet are on the edge of a precipice; Hope flying on forward wings beckons me to follow her, and rather than resign this cherished creature, I jump though at the peril of my Life.

It may seem a strange assertion, but it is not the less true that I place my happiness in your hands. I wish to give you a suspicion without at first disclosing myself; because it would be a cruel addition to all I otherwise endure to become the object of your contempt and the ridicule of others.

If you feel your indignation rising, if you feel tempted to read no more, or to cast with levity into the fire, what has been written by me with so much fearful inquietitude, check your hand: my folly may be great, but the Creator ought not to destroy his creature. If you shall condescend to answer the following question you will at least be rewarded by the gratitude I shall feel.

If a woman, whose reputation has yet remained unstained, if without either guardian or husband to control she should throw herself upon your mercy, if with a beating heart she should confess the love she has borne you many years, if she should secure to you secrecy and safety, if she should return your kindness with fond affection and unbounded devotion, could you betray her, or would you be silent as the grave?

I am not given to many words. Either you will or you will not. Do not decide hastily, and yet I must entreat you to answer without delay, not because I hate to be tortured by suspense, but because my departure a short way out of town is unavoidable, and I would know your reply ere I go. Address me, as E Trefusis [a pseudonym], 21, Noley Place, Mary le Bonne.

[1816]

You bid me write short to you and I have much to say. You also bade me believe that it was fancy which made me cherish an attachment for you. It cannot be a fancy since you have been for the last year the object upon which every solitary moment led me to muse.

I do not expect you to love me; I am not worthy of your love. I feel you are superior, yet much to my surprise, more to my happiness, you betrayed passions I had believed no longer alive in your bosom. Shall I also have to ruefully experience the want of happiness? shall I reject it when it is offered? I may appear to you impudent, vicious; my opinions detestable, my theory depraved; but one thing, at least, time shall show you that I love gently and with affection, that I am incapable of anything approaching to the feeling of revenge or malice; I do assure you, your future will shall be mine, and everything you shall do or say, I shall not question.

Have you then any objection to the following plan? On Thursday evening we may go out of town together by some stage or mail about the distance of ten or twelve miles, There we shall be free and unknown; we can return early the following morning. I have arranged everything here so that the slightest suspicion may not be excited. Pray do so with your people.

Will you admit me for two moments to settle with you where? Indeed I will not stay an instant after you tell me to go. Only so much may be said and done in a short time by an interview which writing cannot effect. Do what you will, or go where you will, refuse to see me and behave unkindly, I shall never forget you. I shall ever remember the gentleness of your manners and the wild originality of your countenance. Having been once seen, you are not to be forgotten. Perhaps this is the last time I shall ever address you. Once more, then, let me assure you that I am not ungrateful. In all things have you acted most honourably, and I am only provoked that the awkwardness of my manner and something like timidity has hitherto prevented my expressing it to you personally.

Clara Clairmont

Will you admit me now as I wait in Hamilton Place for your answer?

∽

[May 1820]

My dear friend,

… It is to my partiality, to my obstinate determination to treat you with generous confidence that you owe the now being possessed of Allegra. To secure to her the affection of her father I have sacrificed myself entirely, but never was there any idea of a stipulation concerning her visits.

Such has been the whole tenor of my conduct ever since her birth; my object is, and ever will be her happiness …

I am shocked by the threats at the conclusion of your letter. I have said before, you may destroy me, torment me, but your power cannot eradicate in my bosom the feelings of nature, made stronger in me by oppression and solitude. I beg from you the indulgence of a visit from my child because that I am weaker every day and more miserable; I have already proved in ten thousand ways that I have so loved her as to have commanded nay to have destroyed such of my feelings as would have been injurious to her welfare. You answer my request by menacing if I do not continue to suffer in silence, that you will inflict the greatest of evils on my child. You threaten to put her in a convent, to deprive her thus of all domestic affections, destroy every seed of virtue that she may have, to make her the believer of the Catholic faith contrary to the enlightened one she was born in & to banish her for-ever from her native land.

... I am willing to undergo any affliction rather than her whole life should be spoilt by a convent education.

... You have a security in the strength of my affection for my daughter.

EDITH WHARTON
TO MORTON FULLERTON

Edith Wharton (née Newbold) 1862–1937; W. Morton Fullerton 1865–1952

Wonderful were the long secret nights you gave me,
  my Lover,
Palm to palm breast to breast in the gloom.

So wrote American novelist Edith Wharton, following a particularly impassioned liaison at a hotel near Charing Cross station in 1909. As the poem continues, the language of sexual pleasure conjoins with that of spiritual release: receding 'waves of rapture' melt into 'the low beat of the soul'. This affair, stumbled across in middle age, ignited in Wharton new sensations and new intensities of feeling. For several years prior to this, Wharton's respectable yet passionless marriage had been floundering. She spent increasing amounts of time in Paris, where she enjoyed the company of writers and artists. It was here she met Morton Fullerton, an American journalist working for *The Times*. Their romance began in early 1908.

A fervent writer of stories and poetry from a young age, Edith did not fully embark upon her literary career until her mid-thirties. She married Teddy Wharton in 1885, and indulged her interests in European travel, interior design and entertaining. Yet the marriage soon suffered on account of Teddy's worsening mental health. Compared to the muted tones of Wharton's amorous life,

Morton Fullerton's was veritably lurid. In the 1880s he had affairs with both men and women. After moving to France in 1891 he was briefly married to a Portuguese opera singer. When he met Wharton he was being blackmailed by a French actress and was involved in a quasi-incestuous relationship with his cousin and adopted sister. How much Wharton knew of these various entanglements remains unclear, although in a letter of early March 1908 (below) she acknowledges that Fullerton's sexual experience far outstripped her own.

Caddishness notwithstanding, Wharton was evidently enraptured by her lover. In the summer of 1909, when their desire for one another was at its most intense, she writes to Fullerton that he had 'set my whole being free'. Wharton had been born into a wealthy and conservative New York family, and the constraints of this social milieu are enduring themes within her writing. Her relationship with Fullerton enabled her to shrug off some of the constrictive dictums of her upbringing and class: 'You woke me from a long lethargy, a dull acquiescence in conventional restrictions'. So too, the affair enabled a spiritual liberation: 'I feel as though all the mysticism in me, the transcendentalism ... were poured into my feeling for you.'

Alongside such transformative experience, however, Wharton suffered periods of acute confusion: 'sometimes I feel that I can't go on like this: from moments of such nearness ... back into complete *néant* [nothingness] of silence'. Having lavished affection upon her, Fullerton would frequently retreat and his correspondence dry up. Wharton, though, was propelled by desire and a strong sense of self-giving love, and it was not until 1910 that her patience began irreversibly to wane. Her letter of April (below) has a markedly weary tone. After a trying year that saw the ugly unravelling of her marriage, she is saddened by Fullerton's apparent toying with her. She concludes that her life was better before they met.

After this the romance dissipated, although the couple continued to correspond. During the First World War Fullerton served as an officer, while Wharton dedicated herself to relief work. Fullerton went on to work for the French newspaper *La Figaro*. Wharton's literary acclaim grew: she continued to publish novels, short stories, critical works, travel narratives and an autobiography, and to host friends and influential figures in her two beautifully designed houses in France. In one of her letters to Fullerton, Wharton recalls that 'You told me once I should write better for this experience of loving'. Indeed, the affair left its trace upon her writing: not only did she write a number of poems, and even a short piece of erotica, under its immediate influence, but a close appreciation of the subtleties of love and desire permeate both her 1915 novel *The Reef* and her acclaimed *The Age of Innocence*, for which she won the Pulitzer Prize in 1921.

∽

[58 Rue de Varenne]
[Early March 1908]

Dear,

… Do you know what I was thinking last night, when you asked me, & I couldn't tell you? – Only that the way you've spent your emotional life, while I've … hoarded mine, is what puts the great gulf between us, & sets us not only on opposite shores, but at hopelessly distant points of our respective shores … Do you see what I mean?

And I'm so afraid that the treasures I long to unpack for you, that have come to me in magic ships from enchanted islands, are only, to you, the old familiar red calico & beads of the clever trader, who has had dealings in every latitude, & knows just what to carry in the hold to please the simple native – I'm so afraid of this, that often & often I stuff my shining treasures back into their box, lest I should see you smiling at them!

Well! And if you do? It's *your* loss, after all! And if you can't come into the room without my feeling all over me a ripple of flame, & if, whenever you touch me, a heart beats under your touch, & if, when you hold me, & I don't speak, it's because all the words in me seem to have become throbbing pulses, & all my thoughts are a great golden blur – why should I be afraid of your smiling at me, when I can turn the beads & calico back into such beauty – ?

⌒

[Mid-April 1910]

Don't think I am *'fâchée'* [angry], as you said yesterday; but I am sad & bewildered beyond words, & with all my other cares & bewilderments, I can't go on like this!

When I went away I thought I should perhaps hear once from you. But you wrote me every day – you wrote me as you used to *three years ago*! And you provoked me to answer in the same way, because I could not see for what other purpose you were writing. I thought you wanted me to write what was in my heart!

Then I come back, & not a word, not a sign. You know that here it is impossible to exchange two words, & you come here, & come without even letting me know, so that it was a mere accident that I was at home. You go away, & again dead silence. I have been back three days, & I seem not to exist for you. I don't understand.

If I could lean on some feeling in you – a good & loyal friendship, if there's nothing else! – then I could go on, bear things, write, & arrange my life …

Now, *ballottée* [tossed] perpetually between one illusion & another by your strange confused conduct of the last six months, I can't any longer find a *point de repère* [point of reference]. I don't know what you want, or what I am! You write to me like a lover, you treat me like a casual acquaintance!

Which are you – what am I?

Casual acquaintance, no; but a friend, yes. I've always told you I foresaw that solution, & accepted it in advance. But a certain consistency of affection is a fundamental part of friendship. One must know *à quoi s'en tenir* [where one stands]. And just as I think we have reached that stage, you revert abruptly to the other relation, & assume that I have noticed no change in you, & that I have not suffered or wondered at it, but have carried on my life in serene insensibility until you chose to enter again suddenly into it.

I have borne all these inconsistencies & incoherences as long as I could, because I love you so much, & because I am sorry for things in your life that are difficult & wearing – but I have never been capricious or exacting, I have never, I think, added to those difficulties, but have tried to lighten them for you by a frank & faithful friendship. Only now a sense of my worth, & a sense also that I can bear no more, makes me write this to you. Write me no more such letters as you sent me in England.

It is a cruel & capricious amusement. – It was not necessary to hurt me thus! I understand something of life, I judged you long ago, & I accepted you as you are, admiring all your gifts & your great charm, & seeking only to give you the kind of affection that should help you most, & lay the least claim on you in return. But one cannot have all one's passionate tenderness demanded one day, & ignored the next, without reason or explanation, as it has pleased you to do since your *enigmatic change in December*. I have had a difficult year – but the pain within my pain, the last turn of the screw, has been the impossibility of knowing what you wanted of me, & what you felt for me – at a time when it seemed natural that, if you had any sincere feeling for me, you should see my need of an equable friendship – I don't say love because that is not made to order! – but the kind of tried tenderness that old friends seek in each other in difficult moments of life. My life was better before I knew you. That is, for me, the sad conclusion of this sad year. And it is a bitter thing to say to the one being one has ever loved *∂'amour* [with self-giving love].

REBECCA WEST TO H.G. WELLS

Rebecca West 1892–1983;
Herbert George Wells 1866–1946

— ◦≫◦≪◦ —

In 1912, at the age of nineteen, Rebecca West was forging her reputation as a literary critic and social commentator upon the pages of the feminist publication *Freewoman* and the socialist *Clarion*. In an unflinchingly acerbic review of H.G. Wells' novel *Marriage* West accuses the acclaimed author of a 'sex obsession' that amounts to 'the reaction towards the flesh of a mind too long absorbed in airships and colloids'. Such vitriol must have come as a shock to Wells, who aligned himself publicly with the cause of female equality, and whose own romantic life was highly unconventional.

Intrigued by her assessment of him, the forty-six-year-old Wells invited West to lunch at his home. She made quite an impression: 'I had never met anything like her before, and I doubt if there was anything like her before.' Wells' wife, accommodating of her husband's copious affairs, discreetly left the two writers to get acquainted and West recalls how they talked 'with immense vitality and a kind of hunger for ideas' for almost five hours. Their early relationship was vivid, erotic and playful. In their letters Wells addresses West as 'Panther', and he is her 'Jaguar'. In 1914 they had a son together. The affair, vestiges of which can be traced in several of their fictional works, lasted for ten years and proved intellectually and creatively sustaining for both.

Over the course of her career West's repertoire included fiction, literary criticism, political journalism and travel writing. She was lauded for the acuity of her intellect, robustness of her views, and originality of her style. Wells was also prolific in his output. Best known for his works of science fiction and his disarming foresight (predicting, among other things, aerial and atomic weaponry), he also produced realist novels, short stories, works of history, scientific textbooks and essays on politics, government and society.

The letter below relates to an early hiatus in their relationship when, in the spring of 1913, Wells brought their incipient romance to a close. West was appalled at having been passed over in this manner and angrily outlines their incompatibility: he wants 'playful puppies' as companions, rather than the intensity she offers. She accuses him of chasing after excitement yet shirking the emotional fallout ('lighting bonfires' despite a 'dislike of flame'), while she herself is vulnerable, loving and liable to 'burn'. West repeatedly depicts herself as something that burns, smashes and is perilously close to death. Wells is the instigator of such ruination – the destroyer. This characterisation corresponds to West's evolving ideas about the relationship between the sexes. In a 1931 essay she would write that 'Men have a disposition to violence; women have not'. Also apparent is an early instance of her defence of female sexuality, when she accuses Wells of being 'spinsterish' in response to her passion.

Gender and sexual equality remained enduring concerns for West – ones she explored in her novels, advocated for in her journalism, and sought in her own life. In H.G. Wells she found a progressive thinker and sexual libertine, a man who in later life would write that 'sex is as necessary as fresh air'. Yet West longed also for an emotional and practical security that her relationship with Wells could not supply. Her words to a friend upon his death capture the contradictory, flammable essence of their partnership: 'Dear H.G., he was a devil, he ruined my life, he starved me, he was an inexhaustible source of love ... I feel desolate because he is gone.'

∞

Hampstead Garden Suburb, N.W.
[Spring 1913]

Dear H.G.,

During the next few days I shall either put a bullet through my head or commit something more shattering to myself than death. At any rate I shall be quite a different person. I refuse to be cheated out of my deathbed scene.

I don't understand why you wanted me three months ago and don't want me now. I wish I knew why that were so. It's something I can't understand, something I despise. And the worst of it is that if I despise you I rage because you stand between me and peace. Of course you're quite right. I haven't anything to give you. You have only a passion for excitement and for comfort. You don't want any more excitement and I do not give people comfort. I never nurse them except when they're very ill. I carry this to excess. On reflection I can imagine that the occasion on which my mother found me most helpful to live with was when I helped her out of a burning house.

I always knew that you would hurt me to death some day, but I hoped to choose the time and place. You've always been unconsciously hostile to me and I have tried to conciliate you by hacking away at my love for you, cutting it down to the little thing that was the most you wanted. I am always at a loss when I meet hostility, because I can love and I can do practically nothing else. I was the wrong sort of person for you to have to do with. You want a world of people falling over each other like puppies, people to quarrel and play with, people who rage and ache instead of people who burn. You can't conceive a person resenting the humiliation of an emotional failure so much that they twice tried to kill themselves: that seems silly to you. I can't conceive of a person who runs about lighting bonfires and yet nourishes a dislike of flame: that seems silly to me.

You've literally ruined me. I've burned down to my foundations. I may build myself again or I may not. You say obsessions are curable. They are. But people like me swing themselves from one passion to another, and if they miss smash down somewhere where there aren't any passions at all but only bare boards and sawdust. You have done for me utterly. You know it. That's why you are trying to persuade yourself that I am a coarse, sprawling, boneless creature, and so it doesn't matter. When you said, 'You've been talking unwisely, Rebecca,' you said it with a certain brightness: you felt that you had really caught me at it. I don't think you're right about this. But I know you will derive immense satisfaction from thinking of me as an unbalanced young female who flopped about in your drawing-room in an unnecessary heart-attack.

That is a subtle flattery. But I hate you when you try to cheapen the things I did honestly and cleanly. You did it once before when you wrote to me of 'your – much more precious than you imagine it to be – self.' That suggests that I projected a weekend at the Brighton Metropole with Horatio Bottomley. Whereas I had written to say that I loved you. You did it again on Friday when you said that what I wanted was some decent fun and that my mind had been, not exactly corrupted, but excited, by people who talked in an ugly way about things that are really beautiful. That was a vile thing to say. You once found my willingness to love you a beautiful and courageous thing. I still think it was. Your spinsterishness makes you feel that a woman desperately and hopelessly in love with a man is an indecent spectacle and a reversal of the natural order of things. But you should have been too fine to feel like that.

I would give my whole life to feel your arms round me again.

I wish you had loved me. I wish you liked me.

Yours,

Rebecca

Don't leave me utterly alone. If I live write to me now and then. You like me enough for that. At least I pretend to myself that you do.

CONFLICTED AND CONDEMNED LOVE

FRANZ KAFKA TO FELICE BAUER

Franz Kafka 1883–1924; Felice Bauer 1887–1960

Over the course of a single night in September 1912 Czech writer Franz Kafka penned 'Das Urteil' ('The Judgement'), a short story of which he was particularly proud. He dedicated the story to Felice Bauer, a woman he had met six weeks earlier. This tale – which depicts the emotionally deformed relationship between a young man, recently engaged, with his father – was no conventional love offering. But then the relationship between Felice Bauer, a practical-minded and self-sufficient young woman who worked for a manufacturing firm in Berlin, and her sickly, tormented paramour in Prague was far from conventional. Indeed, Kafka's letters are peppered with such foreboding sentiments as 'you will never get unadulterated happiness from me; only as much unadulterated suffering as one could wish for', and unusual endearments: 'If we cannot use arms ... let us embrace with complaints'.

By the time Kafka met Felice at the home of his friend Max Brod in 1912, he was dedicated to a life of writing. This he combined with his job at an insurance company, hence the necessity for nocturnal writing sessions. The couple met seldom over the five years of their correspondence, Kafka frequently citing the demands of his writing and the delicacy of his health as reasons against travelling. Their courtship was thus conducted largely through letters. In the early days this dependence upon letters evidently tormented Kafka: 'how can one hope to hold anyone,' he laments, 'with nothing but words?' He routinely wrote twice a day, and was troubled if Felice did not match his output. A pattern emerges by which, in one letter, he chastises her for neglecting him ('You've had enough of me; there is no other explanation'), only to seek forgiveness in the next ('Stay with me, don't leave me'). It is unclear whether it is with intentional irony that he writes in November 1913 that 'It is quite right that we should stop this madness of so many letters; yesterday I even started a letter on this subject which I will send tomorrow'.

Kafka's letters to Felice, of which there are over five hundred, reveal an ongoing struggle between the lure of emotional and domestic security on the one hand, and his requirements for solitude and the prioritisation of his work on the other. In his letter of 11 November 1912 (below) he explains how destabilising he finds the receipt of her letters and the feelings occasioned by them – so much so that he concludes they must 'abandon it all'. Despite these anxieties the relationship continued and the couple eventually became engaged. In the summer of 1914 Felice's family held a celebratory reception, which Kafka loathed, writing in his diary that he felt 'tied hand and foot like a criminal'. Not long after, following a tense meeting between the couple at the Askanische Hof, a hotel in Berlin, the engagement was called off. In his letter of late October/early November 1914 (below) Kafka enumerates the factors that, as he perceives it, have contributed to this dissolution. In January 1915, with affairs between them still unsettled, he comments bitterly that 'I won't write a lot ... we have not achieved much by way of letters'.

In a letter of February 1913 Kafka had written that 'There are times, Felice, when I feel you have so much power over me that I think you could change me into a man capable of doing the obvious'. Yet, though his love for Felice was great, it was not sufficient to lure Kafka away from his disciplined life centred on his work. He feels, he confesses in a letter of autumn 1913, compelled 'to renounce the greatest human happiness for the sake of writing'. The couple were engaged a second time, in July 1917, but a worsening of his health (he was now suffering from tuberculosis) brought an end to their relationship some months later. Felice went on to marry and have children. Kafka was romantically involved with a number of women during the early 1920s, before his death from TB in 1924. Having achieved little success during his lifetime, the posthumous publication of his uniquely dark and uncanny works established Kafka as a leading figure in twentieth-century literature.

∽

11 November 1912

Fraulein Felice!

I am now going to ask you a favour which sounds quite crazy, and which I should regard as such, were I the one to receive the letter. It is also the very greatest test that even the kindest person could be put to. Well, this is it:

Write to me only once a week, so that your letter arrives on Sunday – for I cannot endure your daily letters, I am incapable of enduring them. For instance, I answer one of your letters, then lie in bed in apparent calm, but my heart beats through my entire body and is conscious only of you. I belong to you; there is really no other way of expressing it, and that is not strong enough. But for this very reason I don't want to know what you are wearing; it confuses me so much that I cannot deal with life; and that's why I don't want to know that you are fond of me. If I did, how could I, fool that I am, go on sitting in my office, or here at home, instead of leaping onto a train with my eyes shut and opening them only when I am with you? Oh, there is a sad, sad reason for not doing so. To make it short: My health is only just good enough for myself alone, not good enough for marriage, let alone fatherhood. Yet when I read your letter, I feel I could overlook even what cannot possibly be overlooked.

If only I had your answer now! And how horribly I torment you, and how I compel you, in the stillness of your room, to read this letter, as nasty a letter as has ever lain on your desk! Honestly, it strikes me sometimes that I prey like a spectre on your felicitous name! If only I had mailed Saturday's letter, in which I implored you never to write to me again, and in which I gave a similar promise ... But is a peaceful solution possible now? Would it help if we write to each other only once a week? No, if my suffering could be cured by such means it would not be serious. And already I foresee that I shan't be able to endure even the Sunday letters. And so, to compensate for Saturday's lost opportunity, I ask you with what energy remains to me at the end of this letter: If we value our lives, let us abandon it all.

Did I think of signing myself *Dein* [Yours]? No, nothing could be more false. No, I am forever fettered to myself, that's what I am, and that's what I must try to live with.

Franz

∽

[Late October/Early November 1914]

As far as I am concerned, Felice, nothing whatever has changed between us in the past 3 months, either for the better, or for the worse ... Actually it had not occurred to me to write to you; the futility of letters and the written word in general had become too apparent at the Askanische Hof; but since my head (even with its aches, above all today) has remained the same, it has not failed to think and dream of you, and the life we lead together in my mind has only occasionally been bitter, most of the time peaceful and happy ...

... Because you were unable to believe the things you heard and saw, you thought there were things that had been left unsaid. You were unable to appreciate the immense power my work has over me; you did appreciate it, but by no means fully. As a result you were bound to misinterpret everything that my worries over my work, and only my worries over my work, produced in me in the way of peculiarities which disconcerted you. Moreover, these peculiarities (odious peculiarities, I admit, odious above all to myself) manifested themselves more with you than with anyone else. That was inevitable, and had nothing to do with spite. You see, you were not only the greatest friend, but at the same time the greatest enemy of my work, at least from the point of view of my work. Thus, though fundamentally it loved you beyond measure, equally it had to resist you with all its might for the sake of self-preservation ...

... In me there have always been, and still are, two selves wrestling with each other. One of them is very much as you would wish him to be, and by further development he could achieve the little he lacks in order to fulfil your wishes ... The other self, however, thinks of nothing but work, which is his sole concern; it has the effect of making even the meanest thoughts appear quite normal; the death of his dearest friend would seem to be no more than a hindrance – if only a temporary one – to his work; this meanness is compensated for by the fact that he is also capable of suffering for his work. These two selves are locked in combat, but it is no ordinary fight where two pairs of fists strike out at each other. The first self is dependent upon the second; he would never, for inherent reasons never, be able to overpower him; on the contrary, he is delighted when the second succeeds, and if the second appears to be losing, the first will kneel down at his side, oblivious of everything but him. This is how it is, Felice. And yet they are locked in combat, and they could both be yours …

What this actually means is that you ought to have accepted it all completely, ought to have realised that whatever was happening here was also happening for you, and that everything the work requires for itself, which looks like obstinacy and moodiness, is nothing but an expedient, necessary partly for its own sake and partly forced on me by the circumstances of my life, so utterly hostile to this work …

… Those hours of the day that I consider to be the only ones lived according to my needs, I spend sitting or lying in these three silent rooms, see no one … and – am not happy, certainly not, and yet content at times at the thought that I am doing my duty, as far as the circumstances permit.

… What … were those fears you kept referring to later in the Tiergarten and which forced you more often into silence than into speech? What were they but dislike of my way of life, as well as indirectly of my intentions, which you could not reconcile with yours, which gave you offence? … Over

and over again, fear. I say fear rather than dislike, but the
two feelings merged. And the things you finally said at the
Askanische Hof, weren't they the eruption of all this? ...
You want an explanation for my behaviour last time, and this
explanation lies in the fact that your fears, your dislike, were
constantly before my eyes. It was my duty to protect my work,
which alone gives me the right to live, and your fears proved,
at least made me fear ... that here lay the greatest danger to my
work ...

... your whole idea about the apartment, what does it
show? It shows you agree with the others, not with me ...
These others, when they get married, are very nearly
satiated ... Not so for me, I am not satiated, I haven't started a
business that's expected to expand from one year of marriage to
another; I don't need a permanent home from whose bourgeois
orderliness I propose to run this business – not only do I not
need this kind of home, it actually frightens me ...

... You must answer, Felice, no matter how much you may
object to my letter ... There were moments during last night
when I thought I had crossed the borderline of madness, and I
didn't know how to save myself ...

Franz

SYLVIA TOWNSEND WARNER
AND VALENTINE ACKLAND

Sylvia Townsend Warner 1893–1978;
Valentine Ackland 1906–1969

On Christmas Day 1930 Sylvia Townsend Warner presented her lover Valentine Ackland with a book in which she had inscribed a quotation: 'I'll stand by you'. This inscription expressed a sentiment, a promise, that carried the two women through four decades of life together. Yet Sylvia's commitment was sorely tested by one particular instance of Valentine's infidelity – her affair with American heiress, Elizabeth Wade White.

Sylvia and Valentine became acquainted in the village of East Chaldon in Dorset, drawn there by the literary community that had grown up around the novelist T.F. Powys. Sylvia, then thirty-six, was scholarly, tall and waspish. In her twenties she had pursued an interest in musicology, before turning exclusively to a career in writing. Valentine, aged twenty-three, also cherished literary ambitions, and wrote poetry. Her appearance was striking: marble-skinned and melancholic, with cropped hair and always immaculately dressed – often in gentleman's tailoring.

In 1930 Sylvia invited Valentine to share her cottage in Dorset. One evening, after a week of living together as companions, they were talking through the partition of their bedrooms. Sylvia, moved by the sadness in Valentine's voice, came to her bedside and embraced her. Both record this pivotal moment in their relationship: Valentine writes of how, suddenly, 'I was holding her and kissing her and we were already deeply in love', while Sylvia recalls simply that 'I got into her bed, and found love there'. From that point forward, a tender, playful and devoted love developed between them. In her autobiography Valentine tells of how 'our lives joined up imperceptibly, all along their lengths'.

The early 1930s saw the couple living for a period in Norfolk, before returning to Dorset. In 1935 they joined the Communist Party, and in 1936 travelled to civil war-torn Spain to lend their support to the Republican cause. Sylvia's career flourished, with the publication of poetry, novels and short stories, while Valentine worked as a left-wing journalist. In 1937 they moved into a Victorian house upon the banks of the River Frome in Dorset. They settled into a happy domesticity; Valentine would fish in the river, and Sylvia avidly tended their garden. During these years Valentine was prone to infidelities, in the face of which Sylvia remained sanguine: 'She was so skilled in love that I never expected her to forego love-adventures'.

Yet 1938 heralded the beginning of a more persistent affair, one that deeply unsettled the finely tuned equilibrium of their relationship. It was through Sylvia that Elizabeth Wade White, a beautiful young woman from New Hampshire, first entered the couple's life. Having met in 1929 in New York, Sylvia and Elizabeth corresponded. Elizabeth came to stay with Sylvia and Valentine for four months in 1938, and it was during this time that Elizabeth and Valentine began an affair. Sylvia tolerated this, even moving into the spare room to accommodate the lovers. In the spring of 1939 the three women travelled to America, and for a brief period set up home together, which proved a disagreeable experience. With the outbreak of war in September, Valentine and Sylvia returned to England, where they involved themselves in war work.

Valentine's affair with Elizabeth was resumed, with renewed vigour, in 1949. Valentine hoped for an amicable ménage à trois, yet the prospect of sharing her home proved too painful for Sylvia and she determined to remove herself to a hotel for the duration of Elizabeth's stay. Valentine, finding herself 'in love with two separate and most alien people', floundered amid competing desires and responsibilities: in a letter of 27 July (below) she expresses how integral Sylvia is to her own being, and insists that the forthcoming separation need not damage or diminish their love. In a letter of 1 September (also below), Sylvia, despite her grief over the situation, counsels Valentine to dedicate herself to 'joy and pleasures' over the forthcoming month, and expresses a deep confidence in their love.

While the affair with Elizabeth rumbled on, in the form of correspondence and the occasional meeting, until the early 1950s, Sylvia and Valentine passed through the crisis point of 1949 and their relationship continued loyal and steadfast. The 1950s and 60s saw Sylvia embark upon ambitious literary projects, while Valentine established an antiques business. Valentine's health worsened over the course of the 1960s and she died at home, of cancer, in 1969. In her diary Sylvia describes, with exquisite sensitivity, Valentine's death and the days that followed: she recalls how, in rereading their early love letters, she is pivoted back into a world of 'blazing love & joy'.

∽

Valentine to Sylvia

Frome Vauchurch, [Dorset]
27 July 1949

... So it is an impasse, and now that the thing I thought possible (some kind of duality) has become totally impossible, I am faced with an apparently inevitable choice: and if it is so, there is no doubt at all but that you and I must – if you will – live our joint life together: and not as a second-best ... For everything that is our love is first-best: it is whole and perfect and even though I have become maimed and so bitterly defrauded you, still because of your truth and integrity (in you and in loving me) it has always kept that quality of being perfect and whole ... But if, when Elizabeth has gone you feel you cannot endure me ... then tell me, and I will go away by myself, for a time or forever: or let you go: or do anything I should that might redeem something for you –

But my Love, I do not think it need be so bad. If you can somehow manage to endure this exile for my sake ... if you can, somehow, draw on me for the infinite love that is all yours, inside me; and draw strength and assurance from it, and know that it is there as it always has been, not one whit diminished in kind or in mass ... if you can only last out this month without getting so ill and tired that you lose touch with me then I do most truly think we shall survive: and by survive I mean in our whole state not diminished and not degraded.

I cannot think it is wrong to want to lie with Elizabeth – except that it hurts you so much. I did not know it would do that. It seems fantastic that I did not but it is true. I never for a moment thought, even when I did think, that you would feel that pang. I cannot ask you to forgive me, my Love ... but because I know your love and love you so profoundly to the depth of my being, I do ask you to bear with me in this return to my body! Bear with me and above all, even in the teeth of this strange infidelity, *trust me*; it is true that I love Elizabeth, but the whole truth – and all the truth I have ever seen and known and all the loves and desires and recognitions of my life, and all my happiness and endeavours to be good (in the sense of being whole) are all planted in you and growing out of you, and have their daily life and light solely from this steady and sure love of you, and your love of me.

Can you make any sense out of this? It is so muddled, but there is truth here, as well as sense and all my heart's life. I should be in front of you asking forgiveness but I am somehow not: I am altogether yours and you know that well: and I hold you most safe, and for ever, inside me.

… And I love you, my Love.

Valentine

∽

Sylvia to Valentine

Frome Vauchurch, [Dorset]
1 September 1949

My Love

… O My Love, do not doubt, do not fear. You shall be freed. By your own strength, I trust and believe, and if not, then by mine, which for you is limitless, and which is yours, really, since our love gives it to me. Rely on this, rest on it; and so, feel enabled to be happy, to roll on joy and pleasures as securely as though they were casks. Joy is an innocent thing, when time blows through it and keeps it sweet, it is only when crumpled into a possession that it grows sour. And there is no malice in the body, that brief imperilled creature, that for all the misunderstanding and scorn and ill-usage that mankind lays on it, is still good, willing, artless, enduring all things, hoping all things, and surely much more congenial to God than St. Paul could be.

If you can roll so, then everything will be much better and easier than we dare think. Only today I read in la Bruyère that love grows by kindness but passion is fuelled by vexation and crosses. I do not think that what you have done is very wrong. It is only very dangerous, like a sudden change of diet or of climate. Five months ago we were thrown into a burning fiery furnace; but now it seems to me that we were walking in the midst of it, and that, hand in hand. And so, my love, I think we shall be able to walk out, neither pulling the other, but together, and step for step.

Take care of yourself, my Love. More than I will allow myself to think, depends on that. Trust me. Trust my strength to come to your help, and trust my weakness, to need your love and cherishing. I am nothing without you, you know that now, it is my comfort that you know it, that you know you are my life as well as my love …

Sylvia

ERNEST HEMINGWAY
AND AGNES VON KUROWSKY

Ernest Hemingway 1899–1961;
Agnes von Kurowsky 1892–1984

In March 1919, recently returned home to Illinois following service on the Italian Front, aspiring writer Ernest Miller Hemingway received a letter from his 'girl'. In this letter nurse Agnes von Kurowsky informs Hemingway that her sentiments towards him have waned. She ends the letter hoping that he will forgive her, and predicting that 'a wonderful career' lies ahead of him.

Hemingway, a volunteer with the ambulance service, arrived in Italy in June 1918. In July he sustained serious leg wounds from shrapnel and was transferred to the Red Cross hospital in Milan where he was cared for by von Kurowsky. A relationship gradually developed between them: they held hands, exchanged notes, and she would arrange to work nights to enable them to spend more time together. By the autumn they had determined to marry, although this was to be postponed until they had both returned to the United States and Hemingway had embarked upon a career and built up some savings.

In her letters of October through to December 1918, written while she was nursing elsewhere in Italy, Agnes playfully bombards Hemingway with endearments – 'you are "Why Girls Leave Home", "The Light of My Existence", "My Dearest and Best"'. Although their relationship likely remained unconsummated, her letters hint at physical intimacy; she writes of 'wishing ... I could put my head on that nice place – you know – the hollow place for my face – & go to sleep with your arm around me'. She reassures him of her devotion – 'don't be afraid I'll get tired of you' – and expresses her impatience to marry: 'I sometimes wish we could marry over here, but, since that is so foolish I must try & not think of it'.

Hemingway left Italy in January 1919, and Agnes's letters soon began to evidence a change of heart. She writes of how 'the future is a puzzle to me'. Then, in the letter of 13 March (below), she openly reveals that she no longer loves Hemingway. She cites their difference in age – she was seven years his senior – as a particularly intransigent obstacle. In a short story based upon this experience Hemingway paraphrases her letter thus: 'She was sorry ... she loved him as always, but she realized it was only a boy and girl love ... She knew it was for the best'. In the final paragraph of her letter Agnes delivers the most painful blow: she is to be married to another man whom she has met since Hemingway's departure. Writing to his good friend William (Bill) Horne, Hemingway tells of how he is left 'smashed' by the news: his ideals have been laid waste, his hopes of future happiness destroyed.

In a reply to his friend's letter, Bill Horne urges Hemingway not to bow to disillusionment or despondency: 'stick to your ideals, man. And work like hell.' And work he did. Following a period as a journalist, Hemingway published his first story collection in 1925 and his first novel in 1926. Yet it was on the publication of his second novel *The Sun Also Rises* that his reputation began to grow. He spent much of the 1920s in Paris, during which time he made friends with literary luminaries such as

Ezra Pound and Gertrude Stein. His passion for the wilderness and traditionally manly pursuits (bull-fighting, deep-sea fishing, big-game hunting) infused his work, as did his continued involvement in war: he worked as a reporter during both the Spanish Civil War and the Second World War. Over the decades Hemingway became one of the most prominent and influential American writers of the twentieth century, famous for his lean and unencumbered style. He was awarded the Nobel Prize for Literature in 1954.

It is debatable to what extent Hemingway's 1929 novel *A Farewell to Arms* draws upon his own wartime experiences. Despite the apparent synergy between autobiography and fiction – in the novel, ambulance driver Frederic Henry and nurse Catherine Barkley fall in love in Italy during the First World War – both Hemingway and von Kurowsky have denied any close resemblance to their relationship. Yet, the letters suggest that one aspect of the real-life affair may have transmuted into fiction – that of romantic illusion. In their letters Agnes recognises that self-delusion helped shape her affections (as she tried 'to convince [herself] it was a real love-affair'), while Hemingway acknowledges that he idealised Agnes. So too, the relationship between Frederic and Catherine is initially portrayed as one of longing after the promise of love. Yet, while this fictional tryst flourishes into something more stable and enduring, Hemingway and von Kurowsky's love affair ultimately crumbled into its illusory components.

Von Kurowsky to Hemingway

Ernie, dear boy,

I am writing this late at night after a long think by myself, &
I am afraid it is going to hurt you, but, I'm sure it won't harm
you permanently.

For quite a while before you left, I was trying to convince
myself it was a real love-affair, because, we always seemed to
disagree, & then arguments always wore me out so that I finally
gave in to keep you from doing something desperate.

Now, after a couple of months away from you, I know that
I am still very fond of you, but, it is more as a mother than as
a sweetheart. It's alright to say I'm a Kid, but, I'm not, & I'm
getting less & less so every day.

So, Kid (still Kid to me, & always will be) can you forgive
me some day for unwittingly deceiving you? You know I'm not
really bad, & don't mean to do wrong, & now I realize it was
my fault in the beginning that you cared for me, & regret it
from the bottom of my heart. But, I am now & always will be
too old, & that's the truth, & I can't get away from the fact that
you're just a boy – a kid.

I somehow feel that someday I'll have reason to be proud
of you, but, dear boy, I can't wait for that day, & it is wrong to
hurry a career.

I tried hard to make you understand a bit of what I was
thinking on that trip from Padua to Milan, but, you acted like
a spoiled child, & I couldn't keep on hurting you. Now, I only
have the courage because I'm far away.

Then – & believe me when I say this is sudden for me, too –
I expect to be married soon. And I hope & pray that after you

have thought things out, you'll be able to forgive me & start a
wonderful career & show what a man you really are.

Ever admiringly & fondly

Your friend

Aggie

⌘

Hemingway to Bill Horne

30 March [1919]

Caro Amico [Dear friend],

It is kind of hard to write it. Especially since I've just heard
from you about how happy you are. So I'll put it off a bit. I
can't write it honest to Gawd. It has hit me so sudden …

… Now having failed miserably at being facetious I'll tell
you the sad truth which I have been suspecting for some time
since I've been back and which culminated with a letter from
Ag this morning.

She doesn't love me Bill. She takes it all back. A 'mistake' –
one of those little mistakes you know. Oh Bill I can't kid about
it and I can't be bitter because I'm just smashed by it. And the
devil of it is that it wouldn't have happened if I hadn't left Italy.
For Christ's sake never leave your girl until you marry her. I
know you can't 'Learn about wimmen from me' just as I can't
learn from anyone else. But you, meaning the world in general,
teach a girl – no I won't put it that way, that is you make love
to a girl and then you go away. She needs somebody to make
love to her. If the right person turns up you're out of luck.
That's the way it goes. You won't believe me just as I wouldn't.

But Bill I've loved Ag. She's been my ideal and Bill I forgot all about religion and everything else – because I had Ag to worship. Well the crash of smashing ideals was never merry music to anyone's ears. But she doesn't love me now Bill and she is going to marry someone, name not given, whom she has met since. Marry him very soon and she hopes that after I have forgiven her I will start and have a wonderful career and everything.

But Bill I don't want a wonderful career and everything. That isn't really fair she didn't write 'and everything' – All I wanted was Ag and happiness. And now the bottom has dropped out of the whole world and I'm writing this with a dry mouth and a lump in the old throat and Bill I wish you were here to talk to. The Dear Kid. I hope he's the best man in the world. Aw Bill I can't write about it. 'Cause I do love her so damned much.

And the perfectest hell of it is that money, which was the only thing that kept us from being married in Italy is coming in at such an ungodly rate now. If I work full time I can average around seventy a week and I'd already saved nearly three hundred. Come on out and we'll blow it in. I don't want the damned stuff now. I've got to stop before I begin feeling bitter because I'm not going to do that. I love Ag too much.

Write me Kid,
Ernie

EDITH PIAF TO DMITRIS HORN
AND LOUIS GÉRARDIN

Edith Piaf 1915–1963; Dmitris Horn 1921–1998;
Louis Gérardin 1912–1982

The diminutive frame of the iconic French singer Edith Piaf belied not only the gravelly abandonment of her voice but also her highly tumultuous life. Deserted by her mother, Piaf, born Edith Gassion, spent her childhood years living with her paternal grandmother in a brothel in Normandy. During her adolescence she toured as a street performer, first alongside her acrobat father and then with another female vocalist. A youthful romance led to the birth of a daughter, who died aged only two. In 1935, at the age of twenty, her talent was recognised by nightclub owner Louis Leplée, who transported her from the Paris streets to the world of cabaret. From that point onwards her singing career flourished, and her stage presence as the tremulous, black-clad 'La Môme Piaf' (little sparrow) was born.

Yet success did not guarantee peace. Piaf's personal life unfolded as a passionate swirl of aborted love affairs, loss, addiction and ill-health. Her many lovers included lyricist Raymond Asso, composer Henri Contet, actor Paul Meurisse and musician Jean-Louis Jaubert. Her amours were often intense and short-lived. As expressed in one of her best-known songs, 'La Vie en Rose', Piaf was a woman in the thrall of love, a captive to its transforming power:

Hold me close and hold me fast
The magic spell you cast
This is la vie en rose

...

When you press me to your heart
I'm in a world apart
A world where roses bloom

Her immense capacity to love, and her yearning to be loved, are intimately revealed through the letters she penned.

Piaf met Greek actor Dmitris Horn during a European tour in 1946. He was six years her junior, and still early in a career which would bring him renown on both stage and screen. They spent three romance-drenched weeks together in Athens, wandering through the Acropolis by moonlight and even speaking of marriage. In her four-page letter of September that year (the first page of which is included below), Piaf opens her heart to her 'Taki'. She describes her love for him as overpowering, 'terrible', something over which she has no control. She is desperate to see him, urging him to come to America, then Paris. Piaf was used to quickly installing her lovers in her home, and clearly wished the same for Horn. Yet there is a desperate quality to this letter that suggests she knows her plans are in vain: she speaks of sacrificing all for him, and urges him not to 'break [her] heart'. Horn was a womaniser, and may not have attached such weight to the relationship as did Piaf. In a telegram marked 'urgent', sent two months after the letter, she begs him to write. Yet despite such appeals, the relationship did not last.

Two years later Piaf embarked upon a passionate romance with boxing champion Marcel Cerdan. Considered her greatest love affair, the relationship ended in tragedy when Cerdan was killed in a plane crash. Devastated by this loss, and having been prescribed morphine following a car accident, Piaf entered a period of drug and alcohol abuse. When, in 1951, she met Louis Gérardin, the beautiful blond-haired cycling champion, he struck her as a saviour of sorts. Their relationship lasted less than a year, during which time she sent him over fifty letters full of yearning and devotion. She writes tenderly that 'you have taken me like no man has ever done', refers to herself as his 'little pet dog', and tells of her desire to set up home with him. Yet Gérardin was married and it is again likely that Piaf was the more wildly committed of the two. Nonetheless, it was Piaf who ultimately ended the relationship, having fallen in love with another man, Jacques Pills. In her letter of September 1952 she informs Gérardin that she is soon to be married, and proffers a gentle rebuke for his apathy – she had 'warned' him he might lose her.

Over the course of the 1940s and 50s Piaf's fame grew: she won the hearts of an initially frosty American audience, and remained the darling of her French fans. Yet increasingly her health suffered and money dwindled. It was towards the end of her career, in 1959, that the composer Charles Dumont and lyricist Michel Vaucaire approached her with a new song, 'Non, je ne regrette rien' – a song that captured something of Piaf's own troubled history.

> No, nothing at all
> No, I regret nothing
> Because my life, my joys …
> Today they begin with you.

In her personal life Edith Piaf seemed to have an infinite capacity to begin anew; to shelve old heartaches, disappointments, even grief and enter upon a new romance with all the vigour and intensity of a first love. She is remembered for a voice thick with emotion, and lyrics both sentimental and sorrowful. Vibrating through both her music and her life were the dual themes of love and loss.

∽

Piaf to Horn

Ajaccio

20 September 1946

My Taki

You can't imagine how desperate I am, try as I might to reason with myself it's beyond my control, I need you now and forever and there's nothing I can do. When this terrible love took wing I felt as though everything was collapsing around me, it's impossible to live without one's life, and my life is you. I love you like I've never loved before, Taki, don't break my heart and leave it to die! Perhaps you will come to Paris with Irène, but I don't hold out much hope, so I will come out there to be close to you in November, no one in the world will stop me from coming to Athens, but you must come to America in December, you mustn't hesitate, so that we can be together there, and from there I hope to bring you back with me to Paris, which you will love as much as I do when you get to know it, if you go to London after America I'll go with you, I want to be so close to you, I know I could make you so very happy and I think I understand you so terribly well. I know that I will be able to sacrifice everything for you …

∽

Piaf to Gérardin

New York

18 September 1952

Toto

By the time this letter reaches you I shall be married, and I must be honest with both Jacques and yourself, I am happy to be getting married and do so with all my heart. I have warned you a thousand times that you were going to lose me but you have never responded, and so what was bound to happen has happened: in the end, when you share your life so closely with someone who is tender, kind and so very attentive, you get caught up, and I confess I love Jacques sincerely! I have no wish to dwell on that subject, or on us: what else is to be done in the face of the facts? You took your risks, you were warned by all of your friends and ours, but you wouldn't listen! I want with all my heart not to cause you pain, I know you are strong and a man! I hope with all my heart that I can still be your friend!

I hardly dare ask for a letter from you: I understand too well how hard it will be to write to me, I don't want you to hold this against me, every time you have hurt me I have forgiven you, try to be as generous as I have been!

Nor do I dare touch on the subject of money, as this letter hardly seems the place for it, I leave you to be the judge and know very well that whatever you do with it you will do it well, and if you need it it's there for you and you will pay me back when you are able, for one day I must think a little about myself after all, people have thought of me so little up to now, even those who used to love me. Toto, I would so like to be your friend still and you know that whatever happens you can count on me! For the last time I sign myself:

Your little one

RICHARD BURTON
AND ELIZABETH TAYLOR

Richard Burton 1925–1984;
Elizabeth Taylor 1932–2011

———◦◦◦———

The incendiary love affair between Richard Burton and Elizabeth Taylor famously ignited on the set of *Cleopatra* in 1963. As one screen kiss lingered on, the director Joseph L. Mankiewicz asked politely, 'Would you two mind if I say cut?'. By the early 1960s Taylor, previously a child actress, had unfurled into a sensuous, exceptionally well-paid Hollywood star and Burton, a Welsh miner's son, had established himself as a Hollywood leading man. Before long photographs of the couple were gracing newspapers worldwide. Both already married, they procured divorces and wed in 1964.

Their ten-year marriage was one of professional collaboration (they frequently co-starred in movies), opulence (they bought extravagantly – jewellery, artworks, land, property, a yacht), and passion. In one of his early letters to Elizabeth, Burton writes of how 'I lust after your smell'. At the beginning of their married life Taylor made it clear that she would not tolerate unfaithfulness. Yet during the late 1960s and early 1970s Burton had a number of affairs. His drinking also escalated at this time. Taylor, too, drank heavily and was addicted to painkillers. The couple's arguments, always spirited, increased in ferocity.

By the summer of 1973 Taylor had determined to end their relationship. In an unruly letter of June (below) Burton expresses his sadness and 'wild regret' at the prospect of their split. He underscores his love and regard for his wife, speaking of her 'strange virtues' and talent as an actress and presenting himself as her protector: 'God's eye may be on the sparrow but my eye will always be on you'. In one particularly inebriated-sounding paragraph he lets vent his violent impulses, seemingly directed towards both Taylor's hypothetical future lover and the entire 'ugly' human race.

In July Taylor announced the couple's decision to separate. Yet a health scare (she was hospitalised for stomach pains) drove them back together. On the occasion of their tenth wedding anniversary in March 1974, Taylor jotted a brief note to Burton. In this note (below) she expresses both her 'pure animal' desire for her husband, and her festering anger towards him. That Taylor pointedly refers to Burton as her 'still' husband, and herself as his 'still' wife suggests that she is, at this point – only days before they were to separate for the second time – simultaneously sceptical and hopeful that their relationship will survive.

The couple divorced in June 1974. Then, in October 1975 during a visit to Botswana, they remarried. In his journal Burton records that, although he had reservations about such a move, he loved Elizabeth 'beyond measure and above anything'. Yet by Christmas Burton was pursuing another woman, and in July 1976 he and Taylor once again divorced. In the years that followed Burton continued to act on both screen and stage. Increasingly Taylor focused on work in television, before committing herself to philanthropy, in particular the cause of HIV / AIDS activism, in the

1990s.* Although both Burton and Taylor went on to marry other people (each having two further marriages), they remained close until Burton's death in 1983. Looking back upon their relationship, Taylor reflected that 'from those first moments in Rome, we were always madly and powerfully in love'.

∽

Burton to Taylor

25 June 1973

So My Lumps,

You're off, by God! I can barely believe it since I am so unaccustomed to anybody leaving me. But reflectively I wonder why nobody did so before. All I care about – honest to God – is that you are happy and I don't much care who you'll find happiness with. I mean as long as he's a friendly bloke and treats you nice and kind. If he doesn't I'll come at him with a hammer and clinker. God's eye may be on the sparrow but my eye will always be on you.

Never forget your strange virtues. Never forget that underneath that veneer of raucous language is a remarkable and puritanical LADY. I am a smashing bore and why you've stuck by me so long is an indication of your loyalty. I shall miss you with passion and wild regret.

You know, of course, my angelic one, that everything I (we) have is yours, so you should be fairly comfortable. Don't, however, let your next inamorato use it, otherwise I might become a trifle testy. I do not like the human race. I do not like his ugly face. And if he takes my former wife and turns her into stress and strife, I'll smash him bash him, laugh or crash him etc. Christ, I am possessed by language. Mostly bad. (Sloshed, d'yer think?) So now, have a good time.

... You may rest assured that I will not have affairs with any other female. I shall gloom a lot and stare morosely into unimaginable distances and act a bit – probably on the stage – to keep me in booze and butter, but chiefly and above all I shall write. Not about you, I hasten to add. No Millerinski Me, with a double M. There are many other and ludicrous and human comedies to constitute my shroud.

I'll leave it to you to announce the parting of the ways while I shall never say or write one word except this valedictory note to you. Try and look after yourself. Much love. Don't forget that you are probably the greatest actress in the world. I wish I could borrow a minute portion of your passion and commitment, but there you are – cold is cold as ice is ice.

Taylor to Burton

15 March 1974

My darling (my still) My husband.
I wish I could tell you of my love for you, of my fear, my delight, my pure animal pleasure of you – (with you) – my jealousy, my pride, my anger at you, at times.

Most of all my love for you, and whatever love you can dole out for me – I wish I could write about it but I can't. I can only 'boil and bubble' inside and hope you understand how I really feel.

Anyway I lust thee,

Your (still) Wife

P.S. O'Love, let us never take each other for granted again!

P.P.S. How about that – 10 years!!

LORETTA YOUNG TO SPENCER TRACY

Loretta Young 1913–2000; Spencer Tracy 1900–1967

———— ◦◦◦◦◦◦ ————

The romance between Loretta Young and Spencer Tracy, two stars of Hollywood's Golden Age, was passionate yet short-lived. By the early 1930s both were poised on the brink of highly successful careers. Young had been introduced early to the world of film; she appeared in her first silent movie at the age of three and signed a contract with a studio aged fourteen. Blessed with a delicate beauty as well as her natural talent as an actress (she had never received any formal training), she routinely commanded the role of leading lady by her twenties. Meanwhile, Tracy had studied at the American National School of Drama and worked as a stage actor before breaking into the film industry. Handsome, yet stockily built and with rugged features, he was a somewhat unconventional leading man. However, his success grew; by 1936 he had won an Academy Award, and his film career lasted for the best part of four decades.

Loretta and Spencer met on set in 1933 while filming the Depression-era love story *A Man's Castle*. Their chemistry was apparent to everyone working on the movie. Spencer was married with two children, but was living separately from his wife. He tended to spend his evenings alone in his hotel room, consoling himself with drink. One evening Loretta, feeling sorry for her down-at-heel co-star, asked him to drive her home. A romance developed between the two who, despite their discretion, were increasingly seen together at glitzy venues and soon attracted tabloid speculation. Yet their relationship was no casual affair; they were both Catholics, frequently attending church and confession together, and their relationship may have remained unconsummated on religious grounds. Loretta's parting letter to Spencer – which reveals how she was still very much in love with him yet felt morally obligated to end their romantic involvement – was written in 1934, likely following a counselling session at her church.

That Tracy was a married man posed an insurmountable obstacle to the continuance of his and Young's relationship; his feelings of guilt and heavy drinking likely played a part in its disintegration, but the dominant cause was one of religious conscience. In the letter below, Loretta finds herself painfully pinioned between her desire and her faith: she misses Spencer greatly and longs for his company, yet perceives their affair as a sin against God. She refers to an event that had happened five years previously – her elopement and brief marriage to actor Grant Withers. Following this painful episode, priest and family friend Father Ward had reprimanded her sternly, and the promise she speaks of is her promise to God to become a virtuous role model for her young female fan base. She also makes a new promise: she asks God to ease her break-up with Spencer, and in return she will relinquish the physical side of their relationship. She implores Tracy to commit, with her, to being 'a good boy, and a good girl'. This phrase captures the moral earnestness, even innocence, of Loretta's letter – while also hinting at the passion that needs their full determination to withstand.

In the years following her relationship with Tracy, Loretta's private life remained tumultuous. A short-lived affair with Clarke

Gable in 1935 led to her becoming pregnant and, due to the strict moral mores of the film industry, she concealed the birth of her daughter. Two further marriages followed. Professionally, Young's film career blossomed, reaching its zenith in 1947 when she received an Academy Award. In total, she made almost one hundred movies. In the 1950s she made the bold move to the fledgling medium of television, where she hosted and acted on *The Loretta Young Show*. Following her retirement from the entertainment industry in the 1960s, Loretta dedicated much time to charitable Catholic causes. Her faith, with which her younger self battled so palpably, remained a constant throughout the sparkling success and personal challenges of her life.

∽

My darling –

First of all I want to tell you again, that you haven't been out of my thoughts for a moment since you left me Tuesday night. The few hours that I haven't been thinking, wondering, and worrying about you, I've been dreaming about you.

As I've already told you I'm writing this to you because when I'm with you & listening to your voice I seem to have little or no logic, or common sense and most certainly no resistance.

I thought the most difficult thing I would have to face in my life, as far as my heart's concerned, happened to me five years ago. Up to last night that was true. Now, if possible my darling I love you even more and therefore I'm frightened even more. Because it seems, the struggle of the past few years has taught me absolutely nothing. Unless I am able at this time

to see you and still live up to a promise I made five years ago.
That promise my darling was simply this. 'If God would see
us through our breaking up, without any serious trouble for
either of us, if He would let me go to sleep just two nights a
week … without crying myself to sleep, and a thousand other
"ifs" which I'll not bore you with now.' That I would never
again under any circumstances allow you (if I could prevent it)
or myself to forget him to the extent of committing a sin. That
is why my darling, it's impossible for us to see each other unless
we can be truthfully and honestly a good boy, and a good girl.

I've already told you, but it's important enough to repeat
it here. It's enough for me, just to be able to look at you and
talk with you and although this may sound stupid to say at this
time I know I could do it, if I had even a tiny bit of help from
you Spencer. I've prayed that you'll think this out with your
whole heart and soul; because it means so terribly much to me.
Be honest with yourself my angel and if you decide that it's an
impossibility for you, I'll understand. Then I'll just go on loving
you in my deepest heart as I have done for this very long time
already.

I have already said a prayer that whatever you decide will
be the right way. I would love to be able to close this note
without saying what I am going to say; but I can't. I've also
said a prayer that you will call me to-morrow night. – I love
you

GRAHAM GREENE
TO CATHERINE WALSTON

Graham Greene, 1904–1991; Catherine Walston, 1916–1978

The introduction between Graham Greene and Catherine Walston was a peculiar one. Catherine, the American wife of British landowner Harry Walston, decided, at the age of thirty, to convert to Catholicism. Moved to do so, in part, by Greene's novel *The Power and The Glory*, she contacted the novelist to ask whether he would be her godfather. So began a lengthy affair, passionate and mired in religious guilt. When they met Greene was in the process of separating from his wife, Vivien, and still entangled with his wartime mistress, Dorothy. Catherine was married and the mother of six, although extra-marital dalliances were an accepted feature of the Walston household. She was beautiful, rich, vivacious and carefree; a tonic to Greene's melancholic character. In *The End of the Affair*, Greene's novel inspired by his relationship with Catherine, the narrator recalls his first sight of the woman who was to become his lover: 'I noticed Sarah, I think, because she was happy'. It was likewise Catherine's vitality that made her so irresistible to Greene.

The affair was one of great intensity. It was conducted at full throttle for five years, from 1946 to 1951, and continued in an abated form until 1957. Their romance unfolded in a variety of locales – Catherine's Oxfordshire home, where Greene was often a guest; a windswept cottage on Achill Isle in the West of Ireland;

Greene's villa on the sun-kissed island of Capri. They also spent time together in London, Rome and Paris. In one of his hundreds of letters to Catherine, Greene yearns for the simple intimacy they enjoyed in Ireland: 'I want to be filling the turf buckets for you & sitting next door working, hearing the clank of washing-up.' He signs off with an expression of desire: 'I kiss you, my dear, here, here – and there.' Greene was frequently troubled by doubts over whether Catherine loved him as completely, as ferociously as he loved her. Their characters differed markedly: while he was greedy for her love and jealous of her other lovers, of which there were many, Catherine was freewheeling and virtually devoid of jealousy.

The letters below were written between 1949 and 1951, and reflect apparent crisis-points in the relationship. The short letter of June 1949 indicates that Greene's affections had overrun the boundaries that Harry was prepared to tolerate. A staid Englishman who doted upon his wife, Harry sought to limit Greene's presence only when the novelist's ardour jeopardised the equilibrium of his home. The letter of December is a tender expression of Greene's dependence upon and dedication to Catherine, a 'wail of self-pity' at being apart from her. In January 1950 his mind turns to the practicalities of their setting up home together, as he seeks to persuade her to separate from Harry. That year Catherine would indeed announce to Harry that she was leaving him. Yet a deep fondness and regard for her husband, combined with a fear of losing her children, prevented her from seeing this through. Harry no longer permitted Greene to visit and in 1951, following the publication of *The End of the Affair* (which Greene dedicated to 'C'), demanded the affair cease. Although the relationship in fact continued for some years, the couple's meetings became increasingly infrequent.

In the letter of August 1951, Greene addresses the same inner conflict that fuels *The End of the Affair* – the struggle between human desire and a will to please God. Catherine and Graham's love for one another was all-consuming, encompassing both body and soul. Yet the conflict between their Catholic faith and their adultery was a source of pain for both. Catherine, in particular, experienced increasing anxiety over the religious implications of their romance, probably under the guidance of Dominican priest Thomas Gilby. Greene's letter was seemingly written in response to a telephone conversation in which Catherine voiced misgivings over continuing their physical relationship. Greene is at pains to persuade her that a simple termination of sexual intimacy is not the answer; abstinence will, he argues, aggravate rather than remedy desire.

Catherine's religious conscience, Harry's displeasure, the passage of time and the strains of separation drew from the romance some of its shattering urgency. Greene suffered acutely on account of periods away from Catherine and her disinclination to leave her husband. Depressive moods, heavy drinking, adventurous travels and new affairs characterised the following years. The 'desert' existence that he writes fearfully of in the August letter gradually opened up around him – a life without Catherine, and one vulnerable to the creeping 'boredom', or depression, that had dogged him since adolescence. In 1954 he wrote to her that 'one longs for you like a medicine that takes away the pain'. Finally surrendering in the late 1950s, the end of their affair did not signal the end of their correspondence. In the final letter she wrote him before her death, Catherine pays a simple tribute to what their relationship meant to her: 'There has never been anyone like you and thanks a lot.'

❧

5 St. James's Street, London

[8 July 1949]

My dear, after all this time have we got to say goodbye. Harry says I am not to speak to you. Is this final?

You always said you would stick to me. I don't know what to do. For God's sake send me a line.

❧

[Paris]

[18 December 1949]

Dear, forgive this letter in advance, a humiliating wail of self-pity that I am ashamed of. But I'm missing you terribly here – the fortnight doesn't seem to have helped & I just feel at the end of my tether, or near it. After Mass I was stupid enough to walk across the river, & I found myself crying in the Tuileries Gardens. I don't know what to do. It was all right yesterday when I spoke to you, but one can't telephone all the time. Then I held you at bay till 3 in the morning drinking with Marie, but one can't go on doing that, though I am going out again with her tonight. You captured Rome & Dublin, & now at the second assault you've captured Paris … My dear my dear. I used to like being alone, but now it's a horror. One thinks of times when we were happy & one tries to shut off thought. It's horrible that one can't be happy thinking of happy times like one can in an ordinary relationship.

… I so long for your company – I don't, at this moment, want to make love. I want to sit on the floor with my head resting between your legs like at the Ritz & be at peace. The telephone pulls at my elbow but what's the good? My dear. I never knew love was like this, a pain that only stops when I'm with people, drinking. Thank God, from tomorrow there are lots of engagements.

For God's sake, dear, don't hold this letter against me, & be sweet on Thursday. You can always cure this pain by coming in at the door. You don't know how I need you.

Pray for me.

Graham

∽

5 St. James Street, London
[30 January 1950]

Dear heart,

I'm so sorry that all the trouble has started again. Please remember that I love you entirely, with my brain, my heart & my body, & that I'm always there when you want me.

I don't like or approve of Harry's judgements. When a man marries, he is like a Prime Minister – he has to accept responsibility for the acts of a colleague. My marriage failed (only God can sift all the causes), but the *responsibility* for the failure is mine. One can't lay the blame on one's wife. Your marriage, intrinsically, had failed before I knew you, & the man must accept responsibility – which doesn't mean guilt. It had failed because marriage isn't maintaining a friend, a housekeeper or even a mother. The Catholic service says 'with my body I thee worship', & if that fails the heart has gone out of it.

My dear, any time you say I would lay out a plan of action for living together. I'm certain I could make you happy, & the church would not be excluded. You would be unhappy for a time – that's all, but the division would be over. Harry could not divorce you without your consent & therefore he could not shut down the doors between you & the children. You could insist on sharing them in any separation, just as if I chose I could insist on mine. He is not legally in a position to lay down terms or a way of life for you.

Dear, this letter may make you angry. Don't be. I must, at times, present a practical plan. It's the dearest wish I have – the only wish – to have you with me & to make you happy with me. I believe I could do it, after the bad period was over. I love you now so infinitely more than even a year ago. I have great trust, admiration & gratitude (because of the amount of happiness you have given me & patience you have shown during my bad period). I want you to come away with me for six months & test me. That was what Vivien suggested to me – I think in the long term she is proving more generous & more loving than Harry. I'm sorry (& this will anger you) I don't believe in Harry's love for you or anybody, but his small unit of power.

Dear heart … Come with me on the 15th & stay with Binny until you are rested & can sort things out. I'll stay with you & look after you for weeks, months, years, a lifetime. (Strike out the phrase not required!) I want to grow old with you & die with you.

Your lover, who loves you for ever. God bless you & pray for me.

5 St. James's Street, London
[10 August 1951]

My dear,

In this nervous condition, speaking on the telephone, it seems impossible to convey a meaning without over-emphasis or abruptness.

What I want to say is this. A human relationship, like ours has been, is inextricably physical & mental. I have no *real* belief that the physical side is seriously wrong in the particular circumstances, but you will remember that for the last two years I've urged you to go to confession & communion between our meetings. I can see a great benefit in that. Communion might help to reduce the occasions happily. All *that* I would support to the hilt.

I don't however believe that as long as there's strong desire it's possible to tease oneself while we are together without nerves, anger, impatience – all the things that ruin a relationship finally. You know the peace & quiet we had last time in Anacapri. That was only because the relationship was complete …

You say that the last 4½ years have been a fairy tale … The fairy tale you are substituting is one in which one will be afraid to come into the same bedroom, afraid to kiss, afraid to touch you, when we shall be so self-conscious that the body will be always in one's mind because never at peace. I don't know what kind of 'intellectual companionship' we shall get out of that.

… I think the only way to stay together for life is to go back & back to Confession & Communion after every time or period, but I *don't* believe … in the possibility … of suddenly switching a relation onto the unphysical level. We should try, I agree, when we go away together not to think & emphasise in our own minds beforehand what it entails, there are other motives in being together, but a teasing affair of – let's hold out another day, another two days etc, would only *prevent* the physical love from taking the right proportions.

And whatever the Church may say it gives a lot of scope to the individual conscience, & it goes dead *against* my conscience to believe that it hasn't been far better for you & me to have been faithful to one person for four & a half years than to have lived as we were apt to live before.

Dear heart, if all you mean is this: that in the future we should get back to confession & communion as frequently as we can, that we should want to want God's will (which we don't & can't know), then I am with you all the way. I don't question the value of an *eventual* intention, but if we are simply to cut off the whole physical side of loving each other, I can't share the immediate intention & can't go further than praying 'to want to want'. And as I can't share that *immediate* intention, it would be better – if that's in your mind – to cut right away.

I hope & pray you don't because life would be a real desert without you, & God knows what shabby substitutes one would desperately try to find. But try & answer clearly, dear love.

I love you & I want you & I can't separate the two.

God bless you,

Graham

ABELARD AND HÉLOÏSE

Peter Abelard 1079–1142; Héloïse d'Argenteuil (c. 1090–1101)–1164

————— ◦◦◦◦◦◦ —————

The tale of ill-fated romance between renowned twelfth-century philosopher Abelard and his gifted student Héloïse has captured the popular imagination since medieval times. Their story has been celebrated in literature and upon the stage, and letters of the lovelorn have traditionally been left upon the couple's shared tomb.

A precocious scholar, Peter Abelard swept into the Paris schools, disputed voraciously with his tutors, and soon established his reputation as a master of logic. In his mid to late thirties he fell in love with Héloïse, a young woman highly regarded for her learning. Héloïse lived with her uncle, Canon Fulbert, and Abelard soon secured a position as her tutor. The love affair that unfolded between them knew no bounds. In an autobiographical letter to a friend, Abelard recalls how 'We took all opportunities to express to each other our mutual affections ... In the dead of night, when Fulbert and his domestics were in a sound sleep, we improved the time proper for the sweets of love'. Under the guise of their studies, they would retreat to Fulbert's country residence for periods of less covert lovemaking.

By the time their relationship was discovered, Héloïse was pregnant. The couple married in a secret ceremony, yet news of the scandal soon spread. While Héloïse took temporary refuge in the convent at Argenteuil, the deeply vexed Fulbert exacted a heavy revenge upon her husband: one night, a group of Fulbert's men visited Abelard's bedchamber and castrated him. Following this attack, Abelard determined to become a monk and entreated Héloïse to take the veil. Thenceforth, the lovers would be separated by distance and the dictates of monasticism. Some years later Abelard, then Abbot at the ill-disciplined monastery of St. Gildas, was instrumental in establishing the convent of the Paraclete, where Héloïse became Abbess. It is from this period that the letters between them likely date.

Héloïse's letter below is at times fierce, at times tender. She gives vent to her anger at Abelard's 'neglect' since she took her vows. Yet she passionately longs for his presence, reveals that he has infiltrated the most 'inward retreats of [her] soul', and confesses that she is devoted to him, not God. Abelard's reply expresses a more thoroughgoing conflict between religious faith and love: he deeply desires to serve God, but is restless with a 'desperate passion' and cannot free himself from his remembrances of Héloïse. He concludes on a pious note, exhorting Héloïse to commit herself to the religious life.

Despite the finality with which Abelard signs his letter, the correspondence between the couple continued. Abelard became increasingly resolute in his religiosity, and Héloïse reluctantly followed suit. Their later letters concern matters of doctrine and monastic discipline rather than affairs of the heart. Nonetheless, on his death Abelard's body was sent to the Paraclete, and when Héloïse followed him twenty years later her own body was laid with his. Tradition has it that when the grave was opened Abelard's corpse stretched out its arms to receive his Héloïse.

Héloïse to Abelard

... Observe, I beseech you, to what a wretched condition you have reduced me: sad, afflicted, without any possible comfort, unless it proceed from you. Be not then unkind, nor deny me, I beg of you that little relief which you only can give. Let me have a faithful account of all that concerns you ...

... what cannot letters inspire? They have souls, they can speak, they have in them all that force which expresses the transports of the heart; they have all the fire of our passions, they can raise them as much as if the persons themselves were present; they have all the softness and delicacy of speech, and sometimes a boldness of expression even beyond it.

We may write to each other; so innocent a pleasure is not forbidden us ... I shall read that you are my husband, and you shall see me address you as a wife. In spite of all your misfortunes, you may be what you please in our letter ... There I shall read your most secret thoughts; I shall carry them always about me, I shall kiss them every moment; if you can be capable of any jealousy, let it be for the fond caresses I shall bestow on your letters, and envy only the happiness of those rivals. That writing may be no trouble to you, write always to me carelessly, and without study: I had rather read the dictates of the heart than of the brain ...

... I came hither to ruin myself in a perpetual imprisonment, that I might make you live quiet and easy. Nothing but virtue, joined to a love perfectly disengaged from the commerce of the senses, could have produced such effect. Vice never inspires anything like this, it is too much enslaved to the body ... We leave off burning with desire, for those who can no longer burn for us. This was my cruel uncle's notions; he measured my

virtue by the frailty of my sex, and thought it was the man, and
not the person, I loved. But he has been guilty to no purpose.
I love you more than ever. and to revenge myself of him, I will
still love you with all the tenderness of my soul, till the last
moment of my life …

But tell me whence proceeds your neglect of me since my
being professed? You know nothing moved me to it but your
disgrace … Let me hear what is the occasion of your coldness,
or give me leave to tell you now my opinion. Was it not the sole
view of pleasure which engaged you to me? And has not my
tenderness by leaving you nothing to wish for, extinguished
your desires? Wretched *Héloïse*! … When I pronounced my
sad vow … you had my heart, and I had yours; do not demand
anything back: you must bear with my passion, as a thing
which of right belongs to you …

… Why should I conceal from you the secret of my call?
You know it was neither zeal nor devotion which led me to a
cloister … Among those who are wedded to God I serve a man:
among the heroic supporters of the Cross I am a poor slave to
a human passion; at the head of a religious community I am
devoted to *Abelard* only … I am here I confess, a sinner, but one
who far from weeping for her sins, weeps only for her lover …

… I know what obligations this veil lays on me, but I feel
more strongly what power a long habitual passion has over my
heart. I am conquered by my inclination. My love troubles my
mind, and disorders my will. Sometimes I am swayed by the
sentiments of piety which arise in me, and the next moment I
yield up my imagination to all that is amorous and tender …
I had resolved to love you no more; I considered I had made
a vow, taken the veil, and am as it were dead and buried; yet

there rises unexpectedly from the bottom of my heart a passion which triumphs over all these notions, and darkens all my reason and devotion. You reign in such inward retreats of my soul, that I know not where to attack you …

∾

Abelard to Héloïse

… I remove to a distance from your person, with an intention of avoiding you as an enemy; and yet I incessantly think of you in my mind; I recall your image in my memory; and in such different disquietudes I betray and contradict myself … Religion commands me to pursue virtue, since I have nothing to hope for from love. But love still preserves its dominion in my fancy, and entertains itself with past pleasures. Memory supplies the place of a mistress. Piety and duty are not always the fruits of retirement; even in deserts, when the dew of heaven falls not on us, we love what we ought no longer to love. The passions, stirred up by solitude, fill those regions of death and silence … How miserable am I! My misfortune does not loose my chains, my passion grows furious by impotence, and that desire I still have for you amidst all my disgraces, makes me more unhappy than the misfortune itself. I find myself much more guilty in my thoughts of you, even amidst my tears, than in possessing yourself when I was in full liberty. I continually think of you, I continually call to mind that day when you bestowed on me the first marks of your tenderness …

… I flattered myself that when I should see you no more, you would only rest in my memory, without giving any trouble to my mind ... but in spite of severe fasts and redoubled studies, in spite of the distance of three hundred miles which separates us; your image, such as you describe yourself in your veil, appears to me, and confounds all my resolutions.

... I pass whole days and nights alone in this cloister, without closing my eyes. My love burns fiercer, amidst the happy indifference of those who surround me, and my heart is at once pierced with your sorrows and its own. Oh what a loss have I sustained, when I consider your constancy! What pleasures have I missed enjoying! ... The gospel is a language I do not understand, when it opposes my passion. Those oaths which I have taken before the holy altar, are feeble helps when opposed to you. I hear and obey nothing but the secret dictates of a desperate passion ...

... Come, if you think fit, and in your holy habit thrust yourself between God and me, and be a wall of separation. Come, and force from me those sighs, thoughts, and vows, which I owe to him only ... What cannot you induce a heart to, whose weakness you so perfectly know? But rather withdraw yourself, and contribute to my salvation ... Be God's wholly, to whom you are appropriated ... then shall I be indeed a Religious, and you a perfect example of an Abbess.

... To love *Héloïse* truly, is to leave her entirely to that quiet which retirement and virtue afford. I have resolved it; this letter shall be my last fault. Adieu.

MARIE CURIE TO PAUL LANGEVIN

Marie Curie (née Maria Sklodowska) 1867–1934;
Paul Langevin 1872–1946

———◦◦◦◦◦———

Marie Curie's scientific achievements were immense. She discovered two radioactive elements, and was instrumental in developing the theory of radioactivity. For this pioneering work, she won two Nobel Prizes. Such success is particularly remarkable given the obstacles she faced on account of her sex. In the late nineteenth and early twentieth century the international scientific community was dominated by men, and societal expectations still associated women with the home. The bitter furore that surrounded her private life in 1911 brought some of this latent sexual prejudice to light.

Marie Curie, originally Maria Sklodowska, was born in Warsaw. She grew up in Poland, the fifth child of intellectual and patriotic parents. She worked for some years as a governess, before moving to France in 1891 to study at the Sorbonne. In 1895 she married the French physicist Pierre Curie. In 1898 Pierre joined her in her work on uranium rays, and later that year the couple announced the discovery of polonium and radium. In 1903 they were jointly awarded the Nobel Prize for Physics alongside Henri Becquerel. Marie and Pierre had two daughters, Irène and Eve. Following the sudden death of Pierre in an accident in April 1906, a friend recalled how for four years Marie was 'walled in behind her grief'. In the spring of 1910 people noticed a change in her appearance, a lightening of her demeanour. This corresponds with the beginning of her romantic entanglement with Paul Langevin, a former student of her husband. Langevin was a talented physicist and mathematician five years her junior, to whom Marie attributed a 'wonderful intelligence'. Over the years an intimacy developed between them; they taught together, she spent time with his family, and eventually he began confiding in her about his unhappy marriage.

By the summer of 1910 Paul and Marie would meet secretly in an apartment near the Sorbonne, which they referred to as *'chez nous'* (our place). In one letter Marie writes of the 'delicious memory' of their time together: 'I still see your good and tender eyes, your charming smile.' Langevin's wife, Jeanne, soon became suspicious. Known for her violent temper, Jeanne now made threats to kill Marie and accosted her in the street. In the late summer Marie and her family went for a holiday on the Brittany coast. From here she wrote a long letter to Paul, extracts of which are included below, in which she encourages him to separate from Jeanne. At times the letter sounds cold-hearted, as Marie instructs Paul on how best to extricate himself from his wife. She displays a strong animosity towards Jeanne; she is derisory of her morals, temperament, and mothering. Yet the letter also reveals Marie's own jealousy and fearfulness over Jeanne's continuing hold over Paul. She is suspicious of the tactics Jeanne may employ, and is particularly adamant that Paul resist 'ambushes in order to make her [Jeanne] pregnant'. This letter is one of persuasion; in it, Marie fights for her lover's commitment.

Matters escalated in the spring of 1911 when a detective, hired by Jeanne, stole letters written from Marie to Paul. In the autumn Marie, close to a breakdown, attended a prestigious physics conference in Brussels. While there, she received two telegrams: one informed her that she had won the Nobel Prize for Chemistry, the other that Jeanne had made the love letters public. Marie returned immediately to France and was met by a stone-throwing mob outside her house and a vitriolic outpouring against her in the press, which vilified her as a home-wrecker. Members of the scientific establishment also took a hard line: a group of professors banded together to demand that she leave France, and she was discouraged from attending the Nobel Prize ceremony. Her friend Marguerite Borel commented that the outrage would have been far less had Marie been a man. Marie did collect her Nobel Prize in person, but the scandal had taken its toll and her mental and physical health remained poor for much of the following year.

The romance between herself and Langevin did not recover from this period of strain, although they remained friends. In the years that followed Marie continued to enjoy a successful career. During the First World War she set up radiography units for the treatment of soldiers. In the 1920s and early 1930s she toured America, lectured internationally, sat on scientific committees, and founded the Radium Institute in Warsaw. She died in 1934 from the effects of exposure to radiation.

∽

L'Arcouëst, [Brittany]
Late summer 1910

It would be so good to gain the freedom to see each other as much as our various occupations permit, to work together, to walk or to travel together, when conditions lend themselves.

There are very deep affinities between us which only need a favourable life situation to develop. We had some presentiment of it in the past, but it didn't come into full consciousness until we found ourselves face to face, me in mourning for the beautiful life that I had made for myself and which collapsed in such a disaster, you with your feeling that, in spite of your good will and your efforts, you had completely missed out on this family life which you had wished to be so rich in abundant joy.

The instinct which led us to each other was very powerful, since it helped us to overcome so many unfortunate impressions about the very different way in which each of us had understood, organised our private life.

What couldn't come out of this feeling, instinctive and so spontaneous and so compatible with our intellectual needs, to which it seems so admirably adapted? I believe that we could derive everything from it: good work in common, a good solid friendship, courage for life, and even beautiful children of love in the most beautiful meaning of the word.

... Your wife is incapable of remaining tranquil and allowing you your freedom; she will try always to exercise a constraint over you for all sorts of reasons: material interests, desire to distract herself and even simple idleness.

... Don't forget either that you have constant disagreements about the education of the children or the life of the household; they are the same disagreements which have troubled your life since your marriage began and to which I am a complete stranger. A stable regime based on reciprocal liberty ... making it possible for the children to have an atmosphere in which they could breathe, will never exist in your house. If she committed herself to it, she would never be able to keep her promise, being too violent and too used to getting her way by violent means, then also too crude and too devoid of scruples to understand the harm she is doing to her children.

… Even leaving the children, as long as they are young, principally with their mother and her family, would be less bad than … the continual example of a family in a state of war … If the separation took place, your wife would very quickly stop paying attention to her children, who she is incapable of guiding and who bore her, and you could take up little by little the preponderant direction.

… Finally, my Paul, there are not only your children to consider. There is you, your future as a scientist, your moral and intellectual life. All that has been in great danger for some years. All your friends know it, even if they don't know the reasons … All those who love you: Perrin, Weiss, Bernard, Urbain, have been worried about your state for years; I have heard the same thing said by Seignobos. Your students at the College speak with uneasiness of your visible fatigue for whatever reason. You must realise that. You can neither live nor breathe nor work in the atmosphere which you're in.

You haven't been able to work recently except when your wife was in the hospital. I speak of *preparatory reflection* for the paper that you wrote in August. Your family is a milieu of *irresistible, destructive power, and, I believe, altogether exceptional.* You can't live in this family without being manipulated by it to its own purpose, contrary even to the interest of this family, which should value you more than it does. Even your children become in this group an instrument of your oppression *and not at all in relation to their mother, who is too much of an egoist to allow herself to be exploited.*

… It is certain that your wife will not readily accept a separation, because she has no interest in it; she has always lived by exploiting you and will not find that situation as advantageous. What's more, it is in her character to stay, when she thinks that you would like her to go. It is therefore necessary for you to decide, no matter how difficult that is for you, to do all that you can, methodically, to make her life insupportable … the first time she proposes that she could allow you to separate while keeping the children, *you must accept without hesitation* to cut short the blackmail that she will attempt on this subject. It's enough for now that Jean continues to board at the lycée and that you live in Paris … you could go to see your other children at Fontenay or have them brought to the Perrins'; the change wouldn't be so big as you think and *it would certainly be better for everyone*. We could maintain the same precautions we do now for seeing each other until the situation becomes stable.

… But when I know that you are with her, my nights are atrocious, I can't sleep, I manage with great difficulty to sleep two or three hours; I wake up with a sensation of fever and I can't work. Do what you can to be done with it.

Don't ever come down unless she comes to look for you, work late … As for the pretext that you were looking for, tell her that, working late and rising early, you absolutely have need of rest in order to be able to do your work, that her requirement of a common bed unnerves you and makes it impossible for you to have a real rest and that if you perhaps had given in out of lassitude during the vacation, you refuse absolutely to continue and that, if she insists, you will sleep in Paris with Jean.

Do that, my Paul, I beg of you … and don't let yourself be touched by a crisis of crying and tears; think of the saying about the crocodile who cries because he has not eaten his prey; the tears of your wife are of this kind. It is necessary absolutely that she understands that she can expect nothing from you. When she has understood, she will no longer be unhappy, since you will give her the means to live largely as she pleases; she will be able then to look for pleasure and even affection elsewhere and find it.

… Goodbye, my Paul, I embrace you with all my tenderness; I will try to return to work, even though it is difficult, when the nervous system is so strongly stirred up … I await the joy of seeing you with impatience …

OSCAR WILDE TO LORD ALFRED DOUGLAS

Oscar Wilde 1854–1900; Lord Alfred Douglas 1870–1945

—◦◦◦◦—

Velvet-clad and insouciant, Oscar Wilde is best remembered as a flamboyant dandy; a *bon vivant* whose outlandish behaviour, penetrating witticisms and intoxicating conversation scandalised and amused Victorian society in equal measure. Yet, towards the end of his life he cut a very different figure. Living in self-imposed exile in France, impoverished and publicly shamed, he appealed to an old friend: 'tell me of the beauty you have found in life. I live now in echoes and have little music of my own'.

Love was Wilde's undoing. The circumstances that led to his fall from grace stemmed from his all-consuming, though often fraught, romance with Lord Alfred Douglas – or 'Bosie'. The two met in 1891, when Irish-born Wilde was thirty-seven and Douglas twenty-one. Wilde was, by this point, an established literary figure in London, having gained recognition as a writer of poetry and short stories. During the 1880s he had travelled in America and France, and had worked as a lecturer, critic, journalist and editor. Bosie was an undergraduate at Oxford and an aspiring poet who, by the time of their meeting, was familiar with Wilde's story *The Picture of Dorian Gray*, first published in *Lippincott's Monthly Magazine* and widely condemned in the press for its immorality.

Although sexual activity between men was a crime in Victorian Britain, a homosexual subculture thrived among the London intelligentsia. Although married with two children, Wilde had frequent affairs with men and his acquaintance with Bosie soon developed into romance. Wilde's letters to Bosie display the intertwined threads of desire, devotion and despair that characterised their relationship. In early 1893 Wilde praises a sonnet that Bosie has written, and continues 'it is a marvel that those red rose-leaf lips of yours should be made no less for the madness of music and song than for the madness of kissing', while in March of that year he pleads: 'Bosie – you must not make scenes with me – they kill me – they wreck the loveliness of life'. Bosie was often demanding and hot-tempered, given to histrionics and vindictive letter-writing. Yet despite their many rifts, he and Wilde invariably returned to one another.

During the 1890s Wilde made his name as a playwright. A series of society plays were received rapturously in London, culminating in the success of *The Importance of Being Earnest* in the spring of 1895. Yet professional success coincided with private strife. Bosie's father, the notoriously irascible Marquess of Queensbury, sought to bring an end to his son's involvement with Wilde. He wrote venomous letters to Bosie, threatened Wilde at his home, and left a calling card at Wilde's club on which was inscribed: 'For Oscar Wilde posing as a somdomite [*sic*]'. Following this insult Wilde, encouraged by Bosie, brought a charge of criminal libel against Queensbury. This proved to be a disastrous decision: with evidence amassing against him Wilde was forced to drop the libel charge, was bankrupted through legal costs, and was arrested and charged with 'gross indecency'. He was convicted and sentenced to two years' hard labour.

Wilde began his period of incarceration in May 1895, spending brief periods in Newgate, Pentonville and Wandsworth prisons before being transferred, in November, to Reading gaol.

Here, Wilde was permitted some reading material, pen and paper. Between January and March 1897 he wrote a long letter to Douglas. This letter unfolds as a complex expression of pain, bitterness, insight and acceptance. The extracts below, only a small sample of the letter's 50,000 words, are typical of its character as both a highly personal epistle to Douglas, and a philosophic reflection upon the nature of art and human existence. In this letter, Wilde dissects the relationship between himself and Douglas and the circumstances that led him to prison. He analyses their love, harshly critiquing aspects of Bosie's character and conduct, as well as acknowledging his own weaknesses. As the letter progresses, Wilde reflects upon the extensive religious reading he has undertaken, and the altered perception of pleasure, love and sorrow that imprisonment has revealed to him.

Following his release from prison in 1897, and three years before Wilde's early death, he and Bosie were reunited and lived together for a number of months (a situation that ultimately proved untenable). Despite the suffering it had occasioned, during these early post-prison days Wilde clung to their love as a possible source of redemption. In a letter of October he confides in a friend that Bosie is 'witty, graceful, lovely to look at, loveable to be with. He has also ruined my life, so I can't help loving him – it is the only thing to do'.

∽

Dear Bosie, After long and fruitless waiting I have determined to write to you …

Our ill-fated and most lamentable friendship has ended in ruin and public infamy for me, yet the memory of our ancient affection is often with me, and the thought that loathing, bitterness and contempt should for ever take that place in my heart once held by love is very sad to me …

I have no doubt that in this letter in which I have to write of your life and of mine, of the past and the future, of sweet things changed to bitterness and of bitter things that may be turned to joy, there will be much that will wound your vanity to the quick. If it prove so, read the letter over and over again till it kills your vanity … If there be in it one single passage that brings tears to your eyes, weep as we weep in prison where the day no less than the night is set apart for tears … You must read this letter right through, though each word may become to you as the fire or knife of the surgeon that makes the delicate flesh burn or bleed … Do not be afraid. The supreme vice is shallowness. Everything that is realised is right …

I will begin by telling you that I blame myself terribly … In the perturbed and fitful nights of anguish, in the long monotonous days of pain, it is myself I blame. I blame myself for allowing an unintellectual friendship, a friendship whose primary aim was not the creation and contemplation of beautiful things, to entirely dominate my life …

… While you were with me you were the absolute ruin of my Art, and in allowing you to stand persistently between Art and myself I give to myself shame and blame in the fullest degree …

I blame myself again for having allowed you to bring me to utter and discreditable financial ruin … Your insistence on a life of reckless profusion: your incessant demands for money: your claim that all your pleasures should be paid for by me … You demanded without grace and received without thanks …

But most of all I blame myself for the entire ethical degradation I allowed you to bring on me. The basis of character is will-power, and my will-power became absolutely subject to yours ... Those incessant scenes that seemed to be almost physically necessary for you ... your entire lack of any control over your emotions as displayed in your long resentful moods of sullen silence, no less than in the sudden fits of almost epileptic rage ... these, I say, were the origin and causes of my fatal yielding to you in your daily increasing demands ...

... At the one supremely and tragically critical moment of all my life, just before my lamentable step of beginning my absurd [legal] action, on the one side there was your father attacking me with ludicrous cards left at my club, on the other, there was you attacking me with no less loathsome letters ... Between you both I lost my head ... Blindly I staggered as an ox into the shambles ...

...

There is, I know, one answer to all that I have said to you, and that is that you loved me: that all through those two and a half years during which the Fates were weaving into one scarlet pattern the threads of our divided lives you really loved me. Yes: I know you did. No matter what your conduct to me was I always felt that at heart you really did love me ... you loved me far better than you loved anybody else. But you ... have had a terrible tragedy in your life ... Do you want to learn what it was? It was this. In you Hate was always stronger than love. Your hatred of your father was of such stature that it entirely outstripped ... your love of me ...

... Subtly, silently, and in secret, Hate gnawed at your nature, as the lichen bites at the root of some sallow plant ...

When your father first began to attack me ... I saw at once that a terrible danger was looming on the horizon of my troubled days: I told you I would not be a cat's-paw between you both in your ancient hatred of each other ...

... Do you really think that at any period in our friendship you were worthy of the love I showed you, or that for a single moment I thought you were? I knew you were not. But Love does not traffic in a marketplace, nor use a huckster's scales. Its joy, like the joy of the intellect, is to feel itself alive. The aim of Love is to love: no more, and no less. You were my enemy: such an enemy as no man ever had. I had given you my life, and to gratify the lowest and most contemptible of human passions, Hatred and Vanity and Greed, you had thrown it away. In less than three years you had entirely ruined me from every point of view. For my own sake there was nothing for me to do but to love you. I knew, if I allowed myself to hate you, that in the dry desert of existence over which I had to travel, and am travelling still, every rock would lose its shadow, every palm tree be withered, every well of water prove poisoned at its source. Is your imagination wakening from the long lethargy in which it has lain? You know already what Hate is. Is it beginning to dawn on you what Love is, and what is the nature of Love? It is not too late for you to learn, though to teach it to you I may have had to go to a convict's cell.

...

I have lain in prison for nearly two years. Out of my nature has come wild despair; an abandonment to grief that was piteous even to look at: terrible and impotent rage: bitterness and scorn: anguish that wept aloud: misery that could find no voice: sorrow that was dumb. I have passed through every

possible mood of suffering … Now I find hidden away in
my nature something that tells me that nothing in the whole
world is meaningless, and suffering least of all. That something
hidden away in my nature, like a treasure in a field, is Humility.

… When first I was put into prison some people advised
me to try and forget who I was. It was ruinous advice. It is
only by realising what I am that I have found comfort of any
kind. Now I am advised by others to try on my release to forget
that I have ever been in a prison at all. I know that would be
equally fatal … To reject one's own experiences is to arrest
one's own development. To deny one's own experiences is to
put a lie into the lips of one's own life …

… Sorrow, then, and all that it teaches one, is my new
world. I used to live entirely for pleasure. I shunned sorrow
and suffering of every kind. I hated both. I resolved to ignore
them as far as possible, to treat them, that is to say, as modes
of imperfection. They were not part of my scheme of life. They
had no place in my philosophy … But … during the last few
months I have, after terrible struggles and difficulties, been
able to comprehend some of the lessons hidden in the heart of
pain …

I now see that sorrow, being the supreme emotion of which
man is capable, is at once the type and test of all great Art …

… More than this, there is about Sorrow an intense, an
extraordinary reality … For the secret of life is suffering. It is
what is hidden behind everything …

…

I will admit that it is a severe letter. I have not spared
you …

… Deliberately and by me uninvited you thrust yourself

into my sphere, usurped there a place for which you had neither right nor qualifications, and having by curious persistence ... succeeded in absorbing my entire life, could do no better with that life than break it in pieces ...

... You can't wash your hands of all responsibility ... You can't treat all that you have brought upon me as a sentimental reminiscence to be served up occasionally with the cigarettes and *liqueurs* ... Either today, or tomorrow, or some day you have got to realise it ... I have had to look at my past face to face. Look at your past face to face. Sit down quietly and consider it. The supreme vice is shallowness. Whatever is realised is right ....

For yourself, I have but this last thing to say. Do not be afraid of the past. If people tell you it is irrecoverable, do not believe them. The past, the present and the future are but one moment in the sight of God, in whose sight we should try to live ... What lies before me is my past. I have to make myself look on it with different eyes, to make God look on it with different eyes. This I cannot do by ignoring it, or slighting it, or praising it, or denying it. It is only to be done fully by accepting it as an inevitable part of the evolution of my life and character: by bowing my head to everything that I have suffered ... You came to me to learn the Pleasure of Life and the Pleasure of Art. Perhaps I am chosen to teach you something much more wonderful, the meaning of Sorrow, and its beauty. Your affectionate friend

OSCAR WILDE

KATHERINE PARR
AND THOMAS SEYMOUR

Katherine Parr 1512–1548;
Thomas Seymour 1508–1549

———⎯⟨∘≈∘⟩⎯———

'Gentlemen, I desire company, but I have had more than enough of taking young wives' declared Henry VIII to members of his council in 1542. Twice widowed, Katherine Parr was in her early thirties when she became the sixth and final wife of the King. Initially Katherine resisted Henry's advances, for she was already romantically entangled with the dashing Thomas Seymour. Yet Henry's persistence and Katherine's sense of duty overrode her personal inclinations. Intelligent and warm-hearted, she proved an ideal companion: she took a motherly interest in her three stepchildren, Mary, Elizabeth and Edward; she debated matters of religion with her husband, and equipped herself admirably as regent while Henry was away on campaign.

An ambitious and forceful character, Thomas Seymour had enjoyed increasing influence at court since the King's marriage to his sister, Jane Seymour, Henry's third wife. In 1543, to aid the King's suit of Katherine, Seymour was strategically moved abroad as ambassador to the Netherlands, and subsequently obtained senior positions in the military. He returned to court shortly before Henry's death in January 1547, and was thereafter appointed a member of the Regency Council which was to rule on behalf of his nine-year-old nephew, King Edward VI. Thomas's elder brother, Edward, rose to the position of chief councillor and 'Lord Protector of England'.

Despite rumours that Seymour entertained hopes of marrying either Princess Mary or Princess Elizabeth, he soon rekindled his relationship with the now Dowager Queen Katherine. The letters exchanged between them – a selection of extracts from which are included below – indicate, especially on the part of Katherine, a longstanding and sincere affection. In her letter of April 1547, bubbling with impatience, she anticipates Seymour's forthcoming clandestine visit, even promising to meet him at the gate on his arrival. Also conveyed is the couple's determination to marry, which they did secretly in the spring of 1547. The manner in which they sign their letters echoes the words of the wedding vows.

The risks involved in their hasty union, within six months of the King's death, also become apparent in their correspondence. Not only was Katherine expected to adhere to a longer period of mourning, but the possibility that she could be carrying an heir to the throne made marriage a potentially treasonous act. To lawfully marry, Thomas and Katherine required the permission of the King, the Privy Council and the Lord Protector, yet they sought this only after having wed. They faced particular opposition from the Lord Protector, Edward Seymour, and his wife Anne, who disapproved of their relationship. This obstacle is repeatedly broached in their letters. In April Katherine counsels Thomas not to kowtow to his brother, but rather to seek the support of the King.

Having weathered the storm of controversy, the couple's marriage proved both troubled and short-lived. The resentment between the Seymour brothers, and their wives, grew: Anne challenged Katherine's precedence in court, while Thomas envied Edward's influential position. Meanwhile, a growing familiarity between Thomas and the young Princess Elizabeth, who shared the newlyweds' London home, forced the now pregnant Katherine to send her much-loved stepdaughter away. Despite these tensions, the letters from June reveal Thomas's and Katherine's excitement and tenderness towards each other in advance of their baby's arrival (referred to in these extracts as the 'little knave').

Katherine gave birth to a daughter in the summer of 1548. She soon after fell ill and died. The following year, Thomas's reckless scheming to undermine his brother resulted in his execution on the grounds of treason.

∽

Dowager Queen Katherine to Lord Thomas Seymour
[mid-February] 1547

My lord,

I send you my most humble and hearty commendations, being desirous to know how ye have done since I saw you. I pray you be not offended with me in that I send sooner to you than I said I would. For my promise was but once in a fortnight. Howbeit, the time is well abbreviated: by what means I know not, except the weeks be shorter at Chelsea than in other places.

… I would not have you to think that this mine honest goodwill toward you to proceed of any sudden motion or passion. For, as truly as God is God, my mind was fully bent the other time I was at liberty, to marry you before any man I knew. Howbeit, God withstood my will therein most vehemently for a time and, through His grace and goodness, made that possible which seemeth to me most unpossible – that was, made me to renounce utterly mine own will, and to follow His will most willingly. It were too long to write all the process of this matter. If I live, I shall declare it to you myself ...

By her that is yours to serve and obey during her life,
Katherine the Queen KP

✎

Lord Thomas Seymour to Dowager Queen Katherine
[March] 1547

The like humble and hearty recommendations I send your highness that I received ...

... I beseech your highness to put all fancies out of your head, that might bring you in any one thought, that I do think that the goodness you have showed me is of any sudden motion, as at leisure your highness shall know, to both our contentations [satisfactions]. And this, for lack of leisure, being sent for to my lord my brother, I humbly take my leave of your highness. From Saint James in haste, as may appear to you by my hand.

From the body of him whose heart ye have,
T. Seymour

✎

Dowager Queen Katherine to Lord Thomas Seymour

[April] 1547

My lord,

As I gather by your letter delivered to my brother Herbert, ye
are in some fear how to frame my lord your brother to speak
in your favour. The denial of your request shall make his folly
more manifest to the world … I would not wish you importune
for his goodwill: if it come not frankly at the first, it shall
be sufficient once to have required [requested] it, and after,
to cease. I would desire ye obtain the King's letters in your
favour, and also the aid and furtherance of the most notable
of the Council, such as ye shall think convenient: which thing
obtained shall be no small shame to your brother and loving
sister, in case they do not the like.

… When it shall be your pleasure to repair hither, ye must
take some pain to come early in the morning, that ye may be
gone again by seven o'clock, and so I suppose ye may come
without suspect. I pray you, let me have knowledge near night
at what hour ye will come, that your porteress may wait at the
gate to the fields for you. And this, with my most humble and
hearty commendations, I take my leave of you for this time,
giving you like thanks for your coming to the court when I was
there. From Chelsea.

… By her that is and shall be your humble, true,
and loving wife during her life,
Katherine the Queen KP

Lor∂ Thoma∂ Seymour to Dowager Queen Katherine

17 May 1547

… If I knew by what means I might gratify your highness for your goodness to me, showed at our last being together, it should not be slacked to declare mine to you again. And to that intent that I will be more bound unto your highness, I do make request that, if it be not painful to your highness, that once in three days I may receive three lines in a letter from you – and as many lines and letters more as shall seem good unto your highness.

Also, I shall humbly desire your highness to give me one of your small pictures, if you have any left: who, with his [the picture's] silence, shall give me occasion to think on the friendly cheer that I shall receive when my suit shall be at an end …

From him whom ye have bound to honor, love, and such in all lawful things obey,

T. Seymour

❧

Dowager Queen Katherine to Lor∂ Thoma∂ Seymour

[late May] 1547

My lord,

… I was fully bent, before ye wrote, so to frame mine answer to him [Edward Seymour] when he should attempt the matter, as that he might well and manifestly perceive my fantasy to be more towards you for marriage than any other …

… I shall most willingly observe your commandment of writing to you once in three days, thinking myself not a little bound to you, that it hath pleased you too, so to command me. I have sent in haste to the painteress for one of my little pictures …

My lord, whereas you desire to know how ye might gratify my goodness showed to you at your being here, I can require nothing for the same, more than ye say I have, which is your heart and goodwill during your life: praying you to perform that, and I am fully satisfied. When you be at leisure, let me hear from you; I dare not desire to see you for fear of suspicion. I would the world were as well pleased with our meaning as, I am well assured, the goodness of God is. But the world is so wicked that it cannot be contented with good things …

From Chelsea, by her that is yours to serve and obey during her life,

Katherine the Queen KP

∽

Lord Thomas Seymour to Dowager Queen Katherine

9 June 1548

… I do desire your highness to keep the little knave so lean and gaunt with your good diet and walking, that he may be so small that he may creep out of the mouse-hole. And thus I bid my most dear and well-beloved wife most heartily well to fare …

Your highness's most assured and faithful, loving husband,

T. Seymour

∽

Dowager Queen Katherine to Lord Thomas Seymour

[June] 1548

My lord,

… I gave your little knave your blessing, who like an honest man stirred apace after and before … It has stirred these three days every morning and evening, so that I trust when ye come it will make you some pastime. And this I end, bidding my sweetheart and loving husband better to fare than myself …

By your most loving, obedient, and humble wife.

Katherine the Queen KP

FRANKLIN D. ROOSEVELT
TO LUCY RUTHERFURD

Franklin D. Roosevelt 1882–1945;
Lucy Rutherfurd (née Mercer) 1891–1948

———— ∘⌒⌒∘ ————

Democrat Franklin D. Roosevelt, the 32nd President of the United States, is widely regarded as one of America's great leaders. During his long period in office – he served four terms, from 1933 until his death in 1945 – he steered the nation out of the troubled years of the Great Depression and through the Second World War. Born into a distinguished New York family, Roosevelt enjoyed a privileged upbringing and education. While studying at Harvard his fifth cousin, Republican Theodore Roosevelt, became President. In 1905 Franklin married Eleanor Roosevelt, niece of Theodore, and by 1916 they had five children (a sixth having died in infancy).

Franklin Roosevelt entered politics in 1910, winning a seat in the New York State Senate. He was subsequently appointed Assistant Secretary of the Navy in Woodrow Wilson's government in 1913. On account of her husband's rising career, Eleanor faced an overwhelming array of engagements in Washington. In 1913 she hired a social secretary, an efficient and lively young woman named Lucy Mercer. Franklin, by nature outgoing and flirtatious, was immediately attracted to Lucy, who soon found herself attending family dinner parties and yachting trips. Gradually an intimacy developed between them. They embarked upon an affair in 1916, most likely while Eleanor and the children were away on vacation. In the summer of 1917, having left or been dismissed from the Roosevelts, Lucy was appointed to a post in the Department of the Navy.

Eleanor discovered the affair in September 1918 when, unpacking her husband's luggage after he returned from a trip to Europe, she came across a collection of love letters from Mercer. On being confronted with this evidence Franklin expressed his wish to marry Lucy, and Eleanor offered a divorce. However, a combination of factors militated against this: Roosevelt's mother was horrified at the prospect and threatened to cut her son off financially, while political adviser Louis Howie warned of the repercussions for his career. The couple thus determined to remain married, with Eleanor stipulating that they would no longer share a bed and that Roosevelt was to cease all contact with Mercer. In the aftermath of the affair Mercer left Washington and worked as a governess to the children of widower Winthrop Rutherfurd, whom she married in 1920. Yet despite Lucy's marriage and Franklin's promise to Eleanor, the two remained in contact over the following decades.

The early 1920s were challenging years for Roosevelt. In 1921 he contracted polio and was paralysed from the waist down. After a lengthy period of recuperation he re-entered political life in the mid twenties, and successfully ran for Governor of New York in 1928. During these years he and Lucy (now Lucy Rutherfurd) corresponded on seemingly friendly, rather than romantic terms. In the two letters below, Franklin shares family news and keeps Lucy abreast of an important 'venture' he has undertaken: the development of a treatment centre for polio in Warm Springs, Georgia. His proffering of birthday wishes, expressions of sympathy for a miserable summer, and enquiries after Lucy's health suggest a continuing keen concern for his past lover. In 1932 Franklin D. Roosevelt – soon to be popularly referred to as FDR – was elected President. He arranged for Lucy to attend his inauguration in 1933.

Early in his presidency, Roosevelt embarked upon a bold set of policies designed to deliver relief, recovery and reform in response to economic depression. By the late 1930s attention shifted to foreign policy; with the outbreak of the Second World War he aligned himself with the Allies and gradually upped American assistance before entering the war in December 1941. Contact between Rutherfurd and Roosevelt was reinvigorated during the war years. Lucy visited the President on a number of occasions in 1941, her presence being recorded in the White House records under a false name. After the death of Lucy's husband in 1944 the couple met more regularly, assisted by Roosevelt's daughter Anna and his secretary Grace Tully. Lucy attended a number of intimate dinners at the White House around this time.

Although not included here, Lucy's letters to Grace Tully during this period reveal the necessarily surreptitious nature of their communication: the envelopes are marked 'personal and private', and on one occasion refers to the president as 'B', standing for 'Boss'. In one note Lucy expresses gratitude at Grace's willingness to facilitate her contact with the President, and refers also to the help she receives from Anna. Others concern arrangements for an intended trip by Lucy to Roosevelt's retreat in Warm Springs, and expose her anxieties around the controversy her visit could cause.

Mention is also made in these letters to Elizabeth Shoumatoff, an artist friend of Lucy's who will be joining them to paint a portrait of the President. It was while sitting for this portrait, in the company of Rutherfurd, Shoumatoff and two female cousins, that Roosevelt collapsed from a cerebral haemorrhage on 12 April 1945. He died later that day. The precise nature of the relationship between himself and Rutherfurd in these later years – whether it settled into one of friendship or retained an amorous dimension – remains opaque. A strong affection evidently persisted between them. On learning of Rutherfurd's presence at Warm Springs, despite being angered by the deception, Eleanor deemed it appropriate to send Lucy the unfinished portrait of her husband.

∾

Hyde Park, Dutchess County, New York
22 May [1926]

Dear Lucy

I think you may be interested to know of my latest venture – I have bought Georgia Warm Springs, on the 'instalment plan'! And am busily engaged in its development. The chief feature is of course the spring itself which I am convinced has great possibilities for the treatment of infantile paralysis ...

My own legs continued to gain there this summer & on June 16 I go to Marion Mass., to take further exercises, though I will be back in N.Y. once or twice to go to the office. Between now & the 16th I am in N.Y. trying to catch up for lost time.

... It was so nice to hear about you all ... Anna as you know is to be married June 5th & great preparations are in progress – I wish you knew the child – she is really a dear fine person &

I am happy too in Curtis Dall the new son-in-law – doesn't that sound ancient! ...

Very sincerely yours

Franklin D Roosevelt

P.S. A very belated 'many many happy returns of the day'

∽

New York City

15 September 1927

Dear Lucy

What a shame that you have had such a very hospitally summer – and I am only glad that your invalids are all mending ... You can take comfort though in the fact that we even here have also had a thoroughly wet summer – indeed only ten days ago in Dutchess County all the creeks overflowed as never before in history & carried away bridges and houses. We have been at Hyde Park all the time, except for my mid-week visits to N.Y. ... Next week Eleanor and I go to Warm Springs ...

Then about Oct 20th I return to Warm Springs for a month or six weeks as I suppose it is worthwhile to go on with the thing that is more than any other treatment bringing back the leg muscles. The greater part of the country is in the midst of another epidemic of infantile paralysis I am sorry to say – a great many cases in N.Y. and N.J. ... Ohio & Kentucky & Texas all have had outbreaks – We have 40 patients at Warm Springs & many more applications than we have money to take care of. The 'campaign' for funds progresses slowly, but it seems to take weeks to beg even a few thousand dollars, &

I loathe the thought of this begging & will never succeed as a professional money raiser. If in the next few years I can put the Warm Springs Treatment on a permanent & satisfactory basis I shall never again let my enthusiasm run away with me – but shall settle down into a life of leisure! But by that time it will probably be the Poor House –

I do hope that by this time your invalids are well again ... and too that you will have a good trip home – You say nothing of yourself – It means I hope that you have been well – really well –

Sincerely yours
Franklin D Roosevelt

A FINAL WORD

VERA BRITTAIN AND ROLAND LEIGHTON

Vera Brittain 1893–1970; Roland Leighton 1895–1915

———◦◦◦◦◦———

The First World War not only devastated the bodies and minds of myriad young men sent to fight overseas, but maimed the lives of those left behind. A half-century after the war, writer and political activist Vera Brittain recalled the torment she experienced as a young woman waiting for letters from the front: 'Even when the letters came, they were at least four days old; the writers after sending them would have had time to die many times.'

For Brittain, this agony of uncertainty began when her fiancé Roland Leighton was sent to France in March 1915. Roland was a school friend of Vera's brother, whom Vera met and began corresponding with in 1913. He was a highly accomplished student: a prize-winner, head of house, and a colour-sergeant in the Officers' Training Corps. The son of two writers, he was also sensitive, literary-minded and liberal. Vera, meanwhile, was an ambitious young woman with her sights set on Oxford. With the outbreak of war Roland was impatient to enlist. The martial ethos of his elite public schooling had instilled in him a passionate idealism of manliness and warfare. Roland's pressing sense of duty and Vera's ambivalent emotions at the prospect of his service are expressed in the two extracts from letters written in January and February 1915.*

---

* Note that for all letters except those of September 1915, extracts are presented here; in this instance I have omitted the usual ellipses to indicate abridgement.

Roland left for France in March, having just turned twenty and still fresh from the school playing-fields. Some of the peculiar strains of wartime courtship are revealed in the letters of both April and August. In April, Vera expresses her anxiety that her and Roland's very different war experiences (he at the front, she in Oxford) should distance them; she implores him not to shelter her, but to share the grim truths about his life. By this point she had determined to defer her studies and become a nurse, an occupation she welcomed as a way of connecting with Roland. Meanwhile the letters of August, written after Roland's return on a period of leave, illustrate the pain involved in seeing each other briefly and then being forced to part. Travelling to her family home in Buxton and his in Lowestoft, they snatched what moments alone they could: the train journey on which they became engaged; sitting together on a wind-blown cliff-top; and their parting on a crowded London station when 'too angry and miserable to be shy any more, we clung together and kissed in forlorn desperation'.

The two short notes from September 1915 capture the terrifying precariousness of love in wartime. Roland thinks he may go into action soon and hurriedly writes to inform Vera before the posts are stopped. She responds with a 'last word', in which she tries desperately to offer some balm to the gaping prospect that lies before them both. On this occasion their fears proved unfounded. The blow was to fall later that year, on Boxing Day. Vera was staying with her parents in The Grand Hotel in Brighton, awaiting news of Roland's return to England on leave. She received a phone call; it was Roland's sister: Roland had been killed by a sniper on 23 December.

In 1915 the love between Vera and Roland was young, virtually newborn; it was forged under the pressures of war, and had barely time to draw breath before it was extinguished. While at their meetings they were often reserved and physically reticent, their correspondence is intimate – characterised by intellectual enthusiasm and emotional frankness. Yet there creeps into the letters the insidious influence of war; their youth is marred, their love forced to become increasingly worldly. The letters illustrate the strain placed upon their cultural values, romantic ideals and artistic persuasions in the face of mauling violence. Following Roland's death, Vera was left bereft. She sought out what information she could about the circumstances of his death, and was shattered that, amid the pain of a severe abdominal wound, he uttered no last message for her.

This was not the only loss that Vera was to bear during the war. Her brother, Edward, with whom she was very close, was also killed; as were two good friends, Victor Richardson and Geoffrey Thurlow. In her haunting First World War memoir *Testament of Youth*, published in 1933, Brittain seeks to rekindle the lives that were lost to her. The book is an elegy to these four young men. So too, it is a testimony to her wartime experiences as a Voluntary Aid Detachment nurse, and an exploration of her passage from 'provincial young ladyhood' to post-war pacifism. Indeed, Vera Brittain's enduring commitment to pacifism, about which she wrote and for which she lobbied throughout her life, was deeply rooted in these experiences of harrowing personal loss.

Roland to Vera

Lowestoft

31 January 1915

I am very comfortable here, of course: but a rolling stone does not like to be forced to gather moss. I would give anything to be allowed to go to France. Doesn't Lyndall say somewhere that you can get anything you want if you only want hard enough? I feel so ashamed of myself for still being one of the 'gentlemen in England now abed'. I don't think you mean it when you say that you prefer that I should not go.

❧

Vera to Roland

Oxford

2 February 1915

In consideration of your wish to go to France, and of what I might think of you if you had not that wish, I do want you to go, but when finally I come to regarding myself I find it not so easy to make what I ought to desire agree with what I actually do. I am content to think of your departure, so long as it is always going to be, & *is* not.

❧

Roland to Vera

France

20–21 April 1915

It is very nice sitting here now. At times I can quite forget danger and war and death, and think only of the beauty of life, and love – and you. Everything is in such grim contrast here. I went up yesterday morning to my fire trench, through the sunlit wood, and found the body of a dead British soldier hidden in the undergrowth a few yards from the path. He must have been shot there during the wood fighting in the early part of the war and lain forgotten all this time. The ground was slightly marshy and the body had sunk down into it so that only the toes of his boots stuck up above the soil. His cap and equipment were just by the side, half-buried and rotting away. I am having a mound of earth thrown over him, to add to the other little graves in the wood.

You do not mind my telling you these gruesome things, do you? You asked me to tell you everything. It is of such things that my new life is made.

∽

Vera to Roland

Oxford

25 April 1915

I received your letter dated April 20th this morning. Yes, tell me all the gruesome things you see – I know that even war will not blunt your sensibilities, & that you suffer because of these things as much as I should if seeing them, – as I do when hearing of them. I want your new life to be mine to as great an extent as is possible, & this is the only way it can – Women are no longer the sheltered and protected darlings of man's playtime, fit only for the nursery & the drawing-room – at least, no woman that you are interested in could ever be just that. Somehow I feel it makes me stronger to realise what horrors

there are. I shudder & grow cold when I hear about them, &
then feel that the next time I shall bear it, not more callously,
yet in some way better –

∽

Roland to Vera

London

24 August 1915

In a way I am glad that I am going back tomorrow. If I cannot
be with you I prefer to be as far away as possible. How much
would I not give to hold you and kiss you again even for a
moment! And not being able to, I feel an insane desire to rush
back to France before I need, and leave all to memory as all
that matters is already left.

I have written to your Father. It is entirely informative – not
interrogative, and merely a brief & slightly formal notification
of what the world is pleased to call our engagement. I
should prefer that the world knew nothing about it; but that
unfortunately is impossible.

∽

Vera to Roland

Buxton

27 August 1915

It seems to me that things are still more unfinished, still more
'left off in the middle' than they were before. The world, of
course, won't think so – but we learnt in those few days that
the farther you go, the farther you see there is to go. I thought

when I saw you off in March that nothing in the world could make me feel more deeply than I did then. I was mistaken.

I thought then that if you kissed me once and we had had even that much of fulfilment, I should be more resigned to whatever cruel thing fate had in store for me. There again I was wrong. Resignation is a thing of the devil; it can't come until one has abandoned the hope that hurts so. So now, because you have kissed me, instead of being resigned, I feel an insane impatience quite unlike anything I have known before 'to be able to hold you & kiss you again even for a moment.' So much so that last night, looking out at the dark earth lying silent beneath the midnight stars, I said in my mind 'Oh Roland! Why ever did you exist! And why do I exist! What have we poor mortals done that we should have to suffer so much pain.'

∽

Roland to Vera

France

23 September 1915

I know nothing definite yet; but they say that all the posts will be stopped very soon.

Hinc illae lacrimae.

'Till life & all …'

∽

Vera to Roland

Buxton

26 September 1915

I am sending this in case it should have a chance of reaching you as a last word before all communication between us is cut off.

And if this word should be 'Te moriturum saluto', perhaps it will brighten the dark moments a little to think how you have meant to Someone more than anything ever has or ever will. That which you have done & been will not be wasted; what you have striven for will not end in nothing, for as long as I live it will be a part of me & I shall remember, always.

Yes, 'till life & all …'

Au revoir.

TED HUGHES TO SYLVIA PLATH

Ted Hughes 1930–1998; Sylvia Plath 1932–1963

The relationship between twentieth-century poets Ted Hughes and Sylvia Plath has long provoked fascination, excited controversy and called forth judgement. In popular memory, vivacious American Plath is associated with a flickeringly fragile mental state, captured in her semi-autobiographical novel *The Bell Jar* and culminating in her suicide in 1963. Meanwhile, Yorkshire-born Hughes is perceived as a brooding and melancholy figure, remembered both for his immense poetic achievements – he held the position of Poet Laureate from 1984 – and for his complicated love life. There has been much conjecture as to the causes and conditions of the breakdown of their marriage, the truth of which resides in the hearts of two people, both now dead. What remains are glimpses into their ill-fated romance, captured in the staggeringly beautiful poetry they left behind.

It was in Cambridge that Hughes and Plath met. In her journal Sylvia describes their now famously energetic first encounter, at the launch party of a journal Hughes was co-editing: 'I was stamping and he was stamping ... and then he kissed me bang smash on the mouth ... And when he kissed my neck I bit him long and hard on the cheek ... blood was running down his face.' The two young poets had clearly made quite an impression on one another, and in his poem '18 Rugby Street' Hughes luxuriates in the memory of their courtship:

You were slim and lithe and smooth as a fish.
You were a new world. My new world.
So this is America, I marvelled.
Beautiful, beautiful America.

After only four months, in June 1956, the couple were married, a small wedding in a registry office in London. Together, over the next five years, they advanced their writing careers, taught and travelled in America, and had the first of their two children. In 1961 they made the move from London to Court Green, a rambling old manor house in Devon. They both loved the house and, alongside their writing, immersed themselves in its upkeep. Ted fashioned a desk for Sylvia out of a plank of elm; Sylvia adorned the sewing machine, the mirror frame, the nursery doorway with painted hearts. Outside, they coaxed potatoes, apples and flowers from their newly acquired land.

The rural peace that the couple had won was, however, short-lived. Compounding whatever strains already existed in their marriage was Hughes' infidelity. Canadian poet David Wevill and his wife Assia, tenants of Ted and Sylvia's London flat, came to stay in Devon in May 1962. Dark-eyed and immaculately groomed Assia, a German-born émigré to Mandate Palestine and then to Britain, was an arresting and fascinating presence. In his poem 'Dreamers', Hughes recalls 'her many-blooded beauty' and 'glittering blackness'. Ted and Assia began an affair, and the following months saw the disintegration of the Hugheses' marriage. Announcing their separation in a letter to his sister, Hughes wrote of his growing feelings of stultification: 'this marriage, house, Sylvia … have seemed just like the dead end of everything', while in August Plath wrote to her mother that 'I simply cannot go on living the ... agonized life I have been living ... I want a clean break, so I can breathe and laugh and enjoy myself again'. The painful autumn of 1962 was a period of unparalleled productivity for Plath when, seated at her desk in the dawn light, she penned the poems that would later appear in *Ariel*. With the coming of winter she moved back to London, renting the top-floor flat of No. 23 Fitzroy Road, once home to W.B. Yeats. It was here, in the early morning of 11 February 1963, that Plath taped shut the door to her children's bedroom, turned on the gas oven, and died.

The publication of *Birthday Letters*, at the very end of Hughes' life, pays testament to the lasting toll taken upon him by the events of 1963. The collection constitutes an elegy to Plath and to their relationship; the poems are acts of tender remembrance, of confession, of analysis, and of mourning. A further poem, 'Last Letter', remained unpublished until 2010. The poem tracks Hughes' own, and what he imagines to be Plath's movements during the final weekend of her life: he tells of receiving a mysterious letter from her; he lays bare the retrospective sordidness of his own actions, in spending the weekend with a lover in the home he had once shared with Plath; he tortures himself with the thought that she tried to call him, the phone ringing repeatedly into an empty room. As the title suggests, this poem is an intimate offering; an explanation, an admission of guilt, an appeal. It is an effort of communion between the living and the dead. In the wake of both marital breakdown and of death, persistent threads of memory and tenderness keep this couple, who had once loved deeply, bound to each other. A 'last letter' from one lover to another, it whispers of the unclear boundaries of both the death of love, and of death itself.

Last Letter

What happened that night? Your final night.
Double, treble exposure
Over everything. Late afternoon, Friday,
My last sight of you alive.
Burning your letter to me, in the ashtray,
With that strange smile. Had I bungled your plan?
Had it surprised me sooner than you purposed?
Had I rushed it back to you too promptly?
One hour later—you would have been gone
Where I could not have traced you.
I would have turned from your locked red door
That nobody would open
Still holding your letter,
A thunderbolt that could not earth itself.
That would have been electric shock treatment
For me.
Repeated over and over, all weekend,
As often as I read it, or thought of it.
That would have remade my brains, and my life.
The treatment that you planned needed some time.
I cannot imagine
How I would have got through that weekend.
I cannot imagine. Had you plotted it all?

Your note reached me too soon—that same day,
Friday afternoon, posted in the morning.
The prevalent devils expedited it.
That was one more straw of ill-luck
Drawn against you by the Post-Office

And added to your load. I moved fast,
Through the snow-blue, February, London twilight.
Wept with relief when you opened the door.
A huddle of riddles in solution. Precocious tears
That failed to interpret to me, failed to divulge
Their real import. But what did you say
Over the smoking shards of that letter
So carefully annihilated, so calmly,
That let me release you, and leave you
To blow its ashes off your plan — off the ashtray
Against which you would lean for me to read
The Doctor's phone-number.

                                        My escape
Had become such a hunted thing
Sleepless, hopeless, all its dreams exhausted,
Only wanting to be recaptured, only
Wanting to drop, out of its vacuum.
Two days of dangling nothing. Two days gratis.
Two days in no calendar, but stolen
From no world,
Beyond actuality, feeling, or name.

My love-life grabbed it. My numbed love-life
With its two mad needles,
Embroidering their rose, piercing and tugging
At their tapestry, their bloody tattoo
Somewhere behind my navel,
Treading that morass of emblazon,
Two mad needles, criss-crossing their stitches,
Selecting among my nerves

For their colours, refashioning me
Inside my own skin, each refashioning the other
With their self-caricatures,

Their obsessed in and out. Two women
Each with her needle.

                              That night
My dellarobbia Susan. I moved
With the circumspection
Of a flame in a fuse. My whole fury
Was an abandoned effort to blow up
The old globe where shadows bent over
My telltale track of ashes. I raced
From and from, face backwards, a film reversed,
Towards what? We went to Rugby St
Where you and I began.
Why did we go there? Of all places
Why did we go there? Perversity
In the artistry of our fate
Adjusted its refinements for you, for me
And for Susan. Solitaire
Played by the Minotaur of that maze
Even included Helen, in the ground-floor flat.
You had noted her—a girl for a story.
You never met her. Few ever met her,
Except across the ears and raving mask
Of her Alsatian. You had not even glimpsed her.
You had only recoiled
When her demented animal crashed its weight

Against her door, as we slipped through the hallway;
And heard it choking on infinite German hatred.

That Sunday night she eased her door open
Its few permitted inches.
Susan greeted the black eyes, the unhappy
Overweight, lovely face, that peeped out
Across the little chain. The door closed.
We heard her consoling her jailor
Inside her cell, its kennel, where, days later,
She gassed her ferocious kapo, and herself.

Susan and I spent that night
In our wedding bed. I had not seen it
Since we lay there on our wedding day.
I did not take her back to my own bed.
It had occurred to me, your weekend over,
You might appear—a surprise visitation.
Did you appear, to tap at my dark window?
So I stayed with Susan, hiding from you,
In our own wedding bed—the same from which
Within three years she would be taken to die
In that same hospital where, within twelve hours,
I would find you dead.
                              Monday morning
I drove her to work, in the City,
Then parked my van North of Euston Road
And returned to where my telephone waited.

What happened that night, inside your hours,

Is as unknown as if it never happened.
What accumulation of your whole life,
Like effort unconscious, like birth
Pushing through the membrane of each slow second
Into the next, happened
Only as if it could not happen,
As if it was not happening. How often
Did the phone ring there in my empty room,
You hearing the ring in your receiver —
At both ends the fading memory
Of a telephone ringing, in a brain
As if already dead. I count
How often you walked to the phone-booth
At the bottom of St George's terrace.
You are there whenever I look, just turning
Out of Fitzroy Road, crossing over
Between the heaped up banks of dirty sugar.
In your long black coat,
With your plait coiled up at the back of your hair
You walk unable to move, or wake, and are
Already nobody walking
Walking by the railings under Primrose Hill
Towards the phone booth that can never be reached.
Before midnight. After midnight. Again.
Again. Again. And, near dawn, again.

At what position of the hands of my watch-face
Did your last attempt,
Already deeply past
My being able to hear it, shake the pillow

Of that empty bed? A last time
Lightly touch at my books, and my papers?
By the time I got there my phone was asleep.
The pillow innocent. My room slept,
Already filled with the snowlit morning light.
I lit my fire. I had got out my papers.
And I had started to write when the telephone
Jerked awake, in a jabbering alarm,
Remembering everything. It recovered in my hand.
Then a voice like a selected weapon
Or a measured injection,
Coolly delivered its four words
Deep into my ear: 'Your wife is dead.'

SOURCES,
COPYRIGHT AND THANKS

CHARLOTTE BRONTË: Originals (in French) held at the British Library. Translations available in *The Love Letters of Charlotte Brontë to Constantin Héger* (printed for private circulation, 1914), accessed at the British Library.

WINSTON CHURCHILL: With thanks to Richard C. Marsh for granting access to Churchill's letter dated 7 September 1905. Churchill's undated letter beginning 'This is what I wanted …' accessed via Seth Keller auction house. Both reproduced with the kind permission of Curtis Brown, London on behalf of the Estate of Winston S. Churchill. © The Estate of Winston Churchill.

IRIS MURDOCH: *Living on Paper: Letters from Iris Murdoch 1934–1995*, ed. Avril Horner & Anne Rowe (Chatto & Windus, 2015). Reproduced with the kind permission of Kingston University. The original letter between Murdoch and Queneau is held at Kingston University, and that between Murdoch and Hicks at Bodleian Libraries, University of Oxford (MSS. Eng. c. 7964–6).

W.B. YEATS: *The Gonne–Yeats Letters 1893–1938*, ed. Anna MacBride White and A. Norman Jeffares (W.W. Norton, 1993).

ANDRE DE DIENES: Letter accessed online via *Stars and Letters*, a repository of letters from Hollywood's Golden Age (starsandletters .blogspot.co.uk; accessed summer 2016). Reproduced with the kind permission of Andre de Dienes LLC.

HENRY VIII: *The Love Letters of Henry VIII to Anne Boleyn*, ed. J.O. Halliwell-Phillipps (Fredonia Books, 2006).

VIRGINIA STEPHEN [WOOLF] AND LEONARD WOOLF: Letter from Virginia to Leonard, 1 May 1912: from *Congenial Spirits*, by Virginia Woolf. Published by Chatto & Windus. Reprinted by permission of The Random House Group Limited; and permission of The Society of Authors as the Literary Representative of the Estate of Virginia Woolf, and Houghton Mifflin Harcourt (USA only). Letter from Leonard to Virginia, 29 April 1912: *Letters of Leonard Woolf*, ed. Frederic Spotts (Bloomsbury, 1992). Reproduced with the kind permission of The University of Sussex and The Society of Authors as the Literary Representative of the Estate of Leonard Woolf. Both letters are held at: Monks House Papers, University of Sussex Special Collections at The Keep.

DAVID HUME: *The Letters of David Hume*, vols I and II, ed. J.Y.T. Greig (Clarendon Press, 1932).

CHARLES DICKENS: *The Love Romance of Charles Dickens: Told in His Letters to Maria Beadnell*, ed. Walter Dexter (The Argonaut Press, 1936).

CLAIRE CLAIRMONT: *With Byron in Love*, ed. Walter Littlefield (J.H. Sears, 1926).

EDITH WHARTON: *The Letters of Edith Wharton*, ed. R.W.B. Lewis and Nancy Lewis (Simon & Schuster, 1988).

REBECCA WEST: *Letters of Note: Correspondence Deserving of a Wider Audience*, ed. Shaun Usher (Canongate, 2013). Reproduced with the kind permission of Peters Fraser & Dunlop (www.petersfraserdunlop.com) on behalf of the Estate of Rebecca West. The original of this letter is held at the Beinecke Rare Book and Manuscript Library, Yale University.

FRANZ KAFKA: *Letters to Felice*, ed. Erich Heller and Jürgen Born (Secker and Warburg, 1974).

SYLVIA TOWNSEND WARNER AND VALENTINE ACKLAND: *I'll Stand By You: Selected Letters of Sylvia Townsend Warner and Valentine Ackland*, ed. Susanna Pinney (Pimlico, 1998). Reproduced with the kind permission of the Sylvia Townsend Warner and Valentine Ackland Estates.

ERNEST HEMINGWAY AND AGNES VON KUROWSKY: *Hemingway in Love and War: The Lost Diaries of Agnes von Kurowsky*, ed. Henry S. Villard and James Nagel (Sceptre, 1989).

EDITH PIAF: Lyrics: 'La Vie En Rose (Take Me To Your Heart Again)', words by Mack David, music by Louiguy. © Copyright 1948 Harms Incorporated/Editions Beuscher Arpege. Chester Music Limited trading as Noel Gay Music Company. All Rights Reserved. International Copyright Secured. Used by permission of Chester Music Limited trading as Noel Gay Music Company. 'Non, Je Ne Regrette Rien', words by Michel Vaucaire, music by Charles Dumont. © S.E.M.I. Letter from Piaf to Gérardin: *Mon Amour Bleu: Letters Inédites*, ed. Cécole Guilbert (Grasset, 2011). Letter from Piaf to Horn: supplied by Vergos Auctions Athens. Both reproduced with the kind permission of the Edith Piaf Estate. Translations by Barbara Mellor.

ELIZABETH TAYLOR AND RICHARD BURTON: Letter from Taylor to Burton: accessed via the Paul Fraser Collectibles website (autumn 2015). Reproduced with the kind permission of The Elizabeth Taylor AIDS Foundation (ETAF) and the Elizabeth Taylor Trust. Letter from Burton to Taylor: *More Letters of Note: Correspondence Deserving of a Wider Audience*, ed. Shaun Usher (Canongate, 2015); *Furious Love*, Sam Kashner and Nancy Schoenberger (JR Books, 2010). Reproduced with the kind permission of the Richard Burton Estate.

LORETTA YOUNG: With thanks to Linda C. Lewis, Christopher Lewis and L. Richard Scroggins for granting access to Loretta Young's letter to Spencer Tracy. Reproduced with the kind permission of Christopher Lewis and L. Richard Scroggins.

GRAHAM GREENE: *Graham Greene: A Life in Letters*, ed. Richard Greene (Little, Brown, 2007). Reproduced with the kind permission of David Higham. © Verdant SA.

ABELARD AND HÉLOÏSE: *Letters of Abelard and Heloise: to which is prefix'd a particular account of their lives, amours, and misfortunes*, extracted from Monsieur Bayle (Joseph Leathley, 1740).

MARIE CURIE: *Marie Curie: A Life*, Susan Quinn (Heinemann, 1995).

OSCAR WILDE: *Complete Works of Oscar Wilde* (HarperCollins, 2003).

KATHERINE PARR AND THOMAS SEYMOUR: *Katherine Parr: Complete Works and Correspondence*, ed. Janel Mueller (University of Chicago Press, 2011).

FRANKLIN D. ROOSEVELT AND LUCY RUTHERFURD: All letters held at the FDR Presidential Library, New York.

VERA BRITTAIN AND ROLAND LEIGHTON: *Letters from a Lost Generation: First World War Letters of Vera Brittain and Four Friends*, ed. Alan Bishop and Mark Bostridge (Little, Brown, 1998). Brittain's letters are reproduced with the kind permission of Mark Bostridge and T.J. Brittain-Catlin, Literary Executors for the Vera Brittain Estate 1970. Roland Leighton's letters are reproduced with the kind permission of David Leighton.

TED HUGHES: 'Last Letter' © Estate of Ted Hughes and reprinted with their permission. The original of 'Last Letter' is held at the British Library. The poem was printed in full in the *New Statesman*, October 2010.

SELECT BIBLIOGRAPHY

In addition to autobiographies, journals, memoirs and biographical studies relating to the various individuals in this book, the following anthologies have proved extremely helpful:

Letters of Note: Correspondence Deserving of a Wider Audience, ed. by Shaun Usher (Canongate, 2013)

More Letters of Note: Correspondence Deserving of a Wider Audience, ed. by Shaun Usher (Canongate, 2015)

Love: A Celebration in Art and Literature, ed. by Jane Lahr and Lena Tabori (Stewart, Tabori and Chang, 1982)

Love Letters: 2000 Years of Romance, ed. by Andrea Clarke (The British Library, 2011)

Love Letters of Great Men, ed. by Ursula Doyle (Macmillan, 2008)

Love Letters of Great Women, ed. by Ursula Doyle (Macmillan, 2009)

Love Through the Ages, ed. by Julia Geddes and Helen Ince (Oxford University Press, 2009)

More Love through the Ages, ed. by Julia Geddes and Anna Merrick (Oxford University Press, 2012)

The Truth About Love: A Collection of Writings on Love through the Ages, ed. by Stephen Siddall and Mary Ward (Cambridge University Press, 2009)

ACKNOWLEDGEMENTS

I would like to extend my sincere thanks to Nira Begum for envisioning this book and to her and Robert Sharman for bringing the finished article to fruition. I thank Barbara Mellor for her work on the Piaf translations and Veronique Faber and Alex Stephens for their research assistance. I am also grateful to a number of friends and colleagues: Lara Feigel, Eleanor Oldershaw, Natasha Periyan, Nicola von Bodman-Hensler, Hannah Crummé, Fariha Shaikh and Philippe Roesle have all provided valuable help and suggestions.

The generous assistance of a large number of individuals, archives, publishing houses and other institutions has proved indispensable. I thank all those who have helped in the process of finding, accessing and gaining permission to use the letters in this book. In particular, thank you to Christopher Lewis and Richard Marsh for providing access to unpublished letters, and Linda Lewis and David Leighton for the personal perspectives they added to my research. More detailed acknowledgements can be found in the 'Sources, Copyright and Thanks' section.

Above all, I wish to thank my family for their kindness and support. My parents, brother, sister-in-law and nieces are constant sources of joy to me. And it is with much gratitude and affection that I acknowledge my loving husband, Nick, and our lovely daughter, Tabitha.